BOOKS BY JANE JACOBS

The Death and Life of Great American Cities
The Economy of Cities

THE
QUESTION
OF
SEPARATISM

Quebec and the Struggle over Sovereignty

THE QUESTION OF SEPARATISM

Jane Jacobs

Random House
New York

The Question of Separatism: Quebec and the Struggle over Sovereignty is based on
the five-part 1979 Massey Lectures given by Jane Jacobs, under the title
"Canadian Cities and Sovereignty-Association," which were aired in
November and December of 1979 as part of the Canadian Broadcasting
Corporation Radio's *Ideas* series. The programs were produced
by Max Allen.
The Massey Lectures were created in honor of the Right Honorable
Vincent Massey, former Governor General of Canada, and were
inaugurated by the Canadian Broadcasting Corporation in 1961 to enable
distinguished authorities to communicate the results of original study or
research on a variety of subjects of general interest.

*Grateful acknowledgment is made to the following for permission to reprint
previously published material:*

Harcourt Brace Jovanovich, Inc., and The Hogarth Press Ltd: Quote from
Between the Acts by Virginia Woolf is reprinted by permission of Harcourt
Brace Jovanovich, The Hogarth Press Ltd and the Author's Literary Estate.

J. D. Morton and the *Globe and Mail:* Excerpt from "Are Mutt and Jeff at
Work?" by J. D. Morton (December 14, 1979), is reprinted by permission
of J. D. Morton and The Globe and Mail.

Oxford University Press: English nursery rhyme is reprinted from *The
Oxford Dictionary of Nursery Rhymes* by Iona and Peter Opie (1951) by
permission of Oxford University Press.

Library of Congress Cataloging in Publication Data

Jacobs, Jane, 1916–
The question of separatism.

Includes index.
1. Québec (Province)—Politics and government
2. Québec (Province)—History—Autonomy and independence
movements. 3. Federal government—Canada. I. Title.
FI053.2.J32   320.9714   80–5268
ISBN 0–394–50981–1

Manufactured in the United States of America

24689753

FIRST EDITION

For Pat,
Mary Ann, Larissa
and Doug,
with love

Acknowledgments

This book incorporates and expands the 1979 Massey Lectures commissioned by the Canadian Broadcasting Corporation, given under the title, "Canadian Cities and Sovereignty-Association." I am indebted to Diane Rotstein for research and editorial assistance, to Max Allen, producer of the lectures, and to Geraldine Sherman, executive producer of CBC Radio *Ideas,* for advice, taste, assistance and the enjoyment of working with them. My greatest gratitude is for a fact: that even though the subject was as contentious as the one I chose, it was possible for Canada's government-owned broadcasting corporation to serve free speech without hint or taint of censorship.

For advice and assistance on this expansion of the lectures I am deeply indebted to my publisher and editor, Jason Epstein.

I thank Decker Butzner, Stephen Clarkson, Kari Dehli, Robert, James and Burgin Jacobs, Douglas Manzer, Doris Mehegan, Alan Powell and the staffs of the Norwegian Trade Commission, the Swedish Trade Commission, the Ontario Ministry of Industry and Tourism, Statistics Canada (counterpart of the U.S. Census Bureau) and the Toronto Public Library for various contributions of data and other information, comments, criticism and general assistance. I am especially grateful to those who found and pointed out factual errors; if any remain, and I devoutly hope they don't, I am of course responsible, as I also am for the opinions expressed.

Contents

ONE
Emotion   3

TWO
Montreal and Toronto   10

THREE
The Secession of Norway from Sweden   26

FOUR
National Size and Economic Development   52

FIVE
Paradoxes of Size   65

SIX
Duality and Federation   78

SEVEN
Sovereignty-Association: Connectors   90

EIGHT
Sovereignty-Association: Independence   107

References   124
Index   129

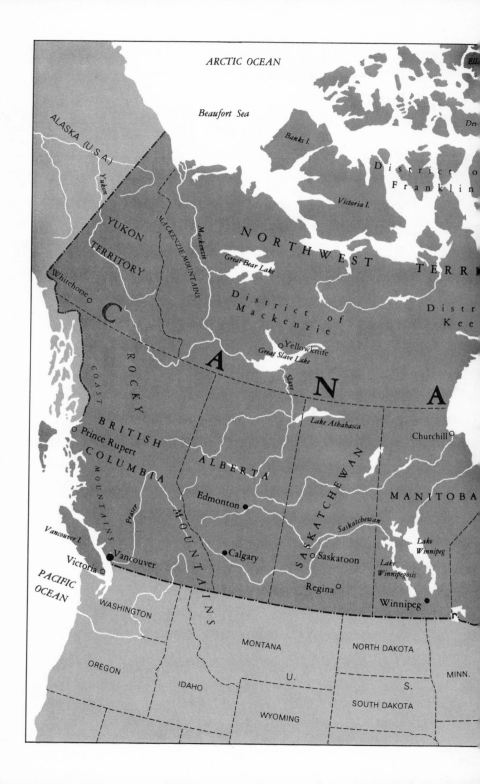

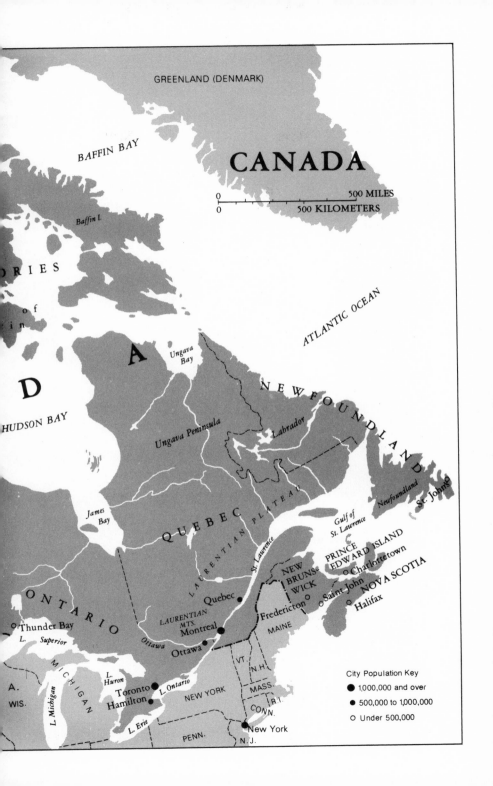

GREENLAND (DENMARK)

BAFFIN BAY

CANADA

500 MILES
500 KILOMETERS

Baffin I.

ORIES

of
in

D A

HUDSON BAY

Ungava
Bay

ATLANTIC OCEAN

NEWFOUNDLAND

Ungava Peninsula

Labrador

James
Bay

QUEBEC

LAURENTIAN PLATEAU

Newfoundland

St. John's

Gulf of
St. Lawrence

St. Lawrence

PRINCE
EDWARD ISLAND

Charlottetown

ONTARIO

LAURENTIAN
MTS.

Quebec

NEW
BRUNS-
WICK

Saint John

NOVA SCOTIA

Thunder Bay

Montreal

Fredericton

Halifax

L. Superior

Ottawa

Ottawa

MAINE

MICHIGAN

L.
Huron

VT.

N.H.

A.

L. Michigan

Toronto

L. Ontario

NEW YORK

MASS.

WIS.

Hamilton

R.I.

L. Erie

CONN.

PENN.

New York

N.J.

City Population Key

● 1,000,000 and over

● 500,000 to 1,000,000

○ Under 500,000

Emotion

It's hard even to think about separatist movements or secessions because the idea is so charged with emotion. Sometimes people literally acknowledge this when they say "It's unthinkable." Nationalist emotions are dangerous, of course. They've helped fuel many a war, many an act of terrorism, many a tyranny. But they are valuable emotions, too. One thing they mean is that we are profoundly attached to the community of which we are part, and this attachment includes for most of us our nation. We care that we have a community. We care how our nation fares, care on a level deeper by far than concern with what is happening to the gross national product. Our feelings of who we are twine with feelings about our nation, so that when we feel proud of our nation we somehow feel personally proud. When we feel ashamed of our nation, or sorrow for it, the shame or the sorrow hits home.

These emotions are felt deeply by separatists, and they are felt equally deeply by those who ardently oppose separatists. The conflicts are not between different kinds of emotions. Rather, they are conflicts between different ways of identifying the nation, different choices as to what the nation is.

3

For separatists in the Canadian province of Quebec, the nation is Quebec. For their opponents, either inside the province or outside it, the nation is Canada-including-Quebec. Canadians who are indifferent to the question of Quebec separatism are likely either to identify primarily with their own province, such as Newfoundland or British Columbia, or else to identify with a Canada which—for all they care emotionally—may or may not include Quebec. That is how I feel about the question. I will not try to justify it as rational, because the fact is that on some level of sheer feeling, not of reason, Quebec seems to me to be already separate and different from what I understand as my own national community. Not that Quebec seems to me inferior, or threateningly strange, or the wrong way for a place to be, or anything of that sort. It's just not my community.

Trying to argue about these feelings is as fruitless as trying to argue that people in love ought not to be in love, or that if they must be, then they should be cold and hard-headed about choosing their attachment. It doesn't work that way. We feel; our feelings are their own argument.

The irrationality of all this shows up in universal patterns of inconsistency. De Gaulle, who said *"Vive le Québec Libre!,"* never said *"Vive la Provence Libre!,"* nor "Long live a free Brittany!" He could feel for separatists abroad but not for separatists at home.

That pattern is usual and ordinary, perhaps always has been. The same Englishmen who ardently favored Greek independence from Turkish rule in the nineteenth century did not therefore also campaign for Irish independence from English rule. Rationally, the one would certainly follow from the other; emotionally, no. British support of Pakistani separatists at the time when India became independent did not imply any comfort or support for Scottish nationalists. Just so, many a

4

Canadian who opposes Quebec separatism was sympathetic to the unsuccessful Biafran secessionist movement in Nigeria. I know some of those people. The same Canadians who can argue eloquently that justice and good sense, both, are on the side of Esthonian, Latvian, Lithuanian, Basque, Croatian, Walloon, Kurdish or Palestinian separatists can maintain that Quebec separatists must be out of their minds to want something unnecessary and impractical.

Separatists are quite as rationally inconsistent themselves. If and when they win their way, they always promptly forget their championship of self-determination and oppose any further separation at home. The colonies that became the United States declared their independence on the grounds that their grievances made it "necessary for one People to dissolve the Political Bands which have connected them with another, and to assume among the Powers of the Earth the separate and equal Station to which the Laws of Nature and of Nature's God entitle them." It has often been remarked how inconsistent that ringing declaration is with the war waged by the Union against the secessionist Confederate States some four score and seven years later.

Today's newly independent nations are one and all against their own separatists or potential separatists. As one student of government* has put it, "Leaders of these new regimes are desperately concerned to argue that self-determination can be employed once in the process of securing independence . . . but that it cannot be resorted to subsequently." Finland, after having achieved independence from Russia in 1918, promptly refused the right of self-determination to Åland, a cluster of islands between Sweden and Finland populated by

*For sources and citations, see references under chapter headings following the text.

ethnic Swedes who sought to join their homeland. Pakistan, having won its own separation, went on to fight the separation of East Pakistan, now Bangladesh. And so on. We may be sure that if Quebec eventually does negotiate a separation, it will oppose adamantly, whether then or thereafter, any separations from Quebec. That is the way all nations behave, no matter how old or young, how powerful or weak, how developed or undeveloped, or how they themselves came into being. But this behavior appears inconsistent only in the light of reason. The consistency is emotional and unreasonable.

These emotions are of course always being presented as reasoned and reasonable, but that does not always stand up to inspection. Take, for instance, the word "Balkanization." Spoken with the ring of authority, "Balkanization" can be made to sound like a compressed history lesson proving the folly of small sovereignties. But what about the Balkans, really?

Before they became small and separate sovereignties, the Balkans had been portions of very large sovereignties indeed, the Turkish and Austro-Hungarian empires. As portions of great sovereignties they had lain poor, backward and stagnant for centuries, so that was their condition when at last they became independent. If a fate called Balkanization has any meaning at all, it must mean that the Balkans were somehow made to be poor, backward and generally unfortunate by having been cut up small, but this is simply untrue. Or else it has to mean that if Rumania, Bulgaria, Yugoslavia and Albania had been joined together in one sovereignty after World War I, or perhaps had been united with Greece to form a still larger sovereignty, they would be better off now. Who knows? In the nature of the thing there is no shred of evidence either to support such a conclusion or to contradict it.

Consider a scholarly-sounding prediction like this one for

Canada if Quebec should separate. "Deprived of real authority or purpose, the federal state would simply disintegrate, like the Austro-Hungarian Empire in 1918." This statement appears in a new work by a professor of political science at the University of Alberta. The trouble with his analogy is that the Austro-Hungarian Empire did not disintegrate as a result of a successful secession. The empire had its separatists, especially in the Balkans, some of whom were violent, but the central authority managed to keep the movements in check. The empire was defeated in a great war, and as it lay prostrate it was deliberately dismembered by the conquerors. The analogy to Canada is so far-fetched historically and so specious factually that we can only understand it rationally as a cry of anguish —not a true account of how things are in Canada, but probably a true account of the depth and desperation of the professor's emotions.

Similar, or even identical, as their underlying themes may be, all separatist movements have their own stories and their own circumstances. In Quebec, separatist sentiment has its old and its new story. The old story began in 1759 when imperial Britain defeated imperial France on the heights above Quebec City during the Seven Years' War, and by right of conquest, ratified by the Treaty of Paris in 1763, took over some 65,000 French colonists who came with the territory.

The conquered Quebecois were not mistreated or notably oppressed in comparison with what has happened to many of history's losers. For instance, unlike the Acadians (French colonists in what has become New Brunswick and Nova Scotia) they were not booted off their lands and driven away. Compared with what happened in Ireland or Scotland, the history of Quebec is a gentle story indeed. Only once, in 1837, did Quebec rebellion or British repression flare into the open. By and large, each partner yielded to the other, even though grudgingly, when it felt compelled to. The English repeatedly made accommodations to French demands for local and provincial self-government, while at the same time hedging against French political power, as it grew provincially, by tying Quebec into a larger government—first into a joint government over Quebec and Ontario, then into the wider Confederation extending finally from sea to sea. For their part, the French repeatedly made their accommodations to English economic schemes, to the use of the English language in industry, commerce and secular higher education, and to the gradually eroding Quebec influence within the national government as English-speaking Canada outstripped Quebec in population and territory.

But even though it was hardly the stuff of high tragedy, the shotgun union of the two Canadas, French and English, proved neither happy nor fruitful. Each partner kept hoping, in vain, to reform the other into something closer to its heart's desire. The English were disappointed by the obstinate refusal of the French to give up their language and customs and assimilate into the society of their conquerors, then became exasperated with the French as priest-ridden, tradition-bound, backward, clannish and occasionally sullen or riotous. The French resented English assumptions of superiority and English mastery over commerce and industry; they felt they were dominated, kept dependent, cheated of equality, threatened with loss of identity. While the mutual accommodations put a reasonably good face on the pain and unhappiness, the accommodations themselves, forced on each partner and begrudged by each partner, tended to become sources of new grievances and to feed resentments.

That was the old story. The new story began about 1960 with what is called the "quiet revolution." One of the partners actually did make itself over. After all those years of sulking and muttering, French Quebec suddenly became outgoing, educated, liberated, and went in for consciousness-raising. Dazzled and alarmed, the other partner tried to make itself over too—took some French lessons, paid compliments and vowed to remove any remaining impediments to harmony.

But curiously enough, in view of so much change for the better, the thought of a separation was not laid to rest. Quebec took to discussing the possibility loudly and openly, right in public. The rest of Canada, by turns irritated and frightened, tried to remember most of the time that least said is soonest mended and told itself that with a little firm treatment, the passage of time, and some no-nonsense talk about economic realities, Quebec would get over its emotional jag or neurosis or instability or whatever this folly was, and surely come to its senses. With so much feeling in the air, nobody was doing much thinking or wondering about whether a logic of events might possibly underlie the new story and might tell more about the new separatism than recitals of the old grievances, the old disdains, the old prides.

TWO
Montreal and Toronto

To understand why sovereignty has emerged as a serious issue in Quebec at this time, we must look at two cities, Montreal and Toronto. They are responsible for what has been happening in Quebec. Between them, they have converted Quebec into something resembling a new nation, provincial political status notwithstanding. Nobody planned this outcome. Nobody even recognized what was happening at the time it happened. The events that worked this transformation do not go back very far. We can date them statistically as having begun in 1941, but that is because 1941 was a census year. I suspect they began in 1939 with the outbreak of World War II and the beginnings of the Canadian war economy.

Let us begin with Montreal. Between 1941 and 1971, Montreal grew enormously. In those thirty years the city more than doubled its population, increasing to more than two million. Immigrants from other countries contributed to Montreal's growth; so did people from other parts of Canada. Of course, some of the growth was natural increase, accounted for by births in the population Montreal already had. But the major influx was from rural and small-town Quebec.

Before, rural Quebecois had migrated to Montreal, just as they migrated to Quebec City and to New England, but this new migration dwarfed previous rural-to-city movements within the province. The rapidity with which the movement happened and the absolute numbers of people involved were unprecedented.

The French-speaking migrants to Montreal spent the 1940s and 1950s finding one another. The "quiet revolution" arose from their networks of new interests and relationships: from new communities of interest and interaction in the city; in the arts, in politics, working life and education. French culture in Montreal was in a quiet ferment as people built these relationships and put together ambitions and ideas they could not have developed even in a smaller city like the capital, Quebec City.

In the 1960s the evidence of this ferment burst forth in French theater, music, films and television. Talent and audiences had found one another. There was a new and rapidly growing readership for Quebecois books and periodicals; writers and readers had also found one another. At about the same time, for a combination of reasons, new kinds of opportunities finally began opening up to Quebecois in city professions and commerce. The most important of those reasons was the sheer economic growth of Montreal, stimulated first by war manufacturing and services, then by an influx of branch plants attracted by the pent-up demands after the war, and by growing trade with other parts of a generally prospering Canada and United States. Montreal maintained a rapid rate of economic growth well into the 1960s, and then kept the exuberant expansion—or a reasonable facsimile of it—going a little longer with special stimulants such as Expo, the Olympics and a variety of ambitious public construction programs.

Until the late 1960s, Montreal still seemed to be what it had been for almost two centuries: an English city containing many

French-speaking workers and inhabitants. But, in fact, by 1960 Montreal had become a French city with many English-speaking inhabitants. By the time people in Montreal, let alone the rest of Canada, recognized what was happening, it had already happened.

Out in rural Quebec, the old stronghold of French culture and customs, another kind of quiet revolution had been taking place. From farming villages, market towns and mill towns, hundreds of thousands of people, especially young people, were trickling and then pouring into Montreal. As the stream swelled it had its effects on French education and aspirations. If one's destination was to be Montreal, there was much to be said for seeking an education and for nourishing ambitions that would have been pointless for one's parents and grandparents.

Life also changed for people who stayed put in rural parishes and villages. The Montreal market for rural goods expanded rapidly. A million extra city people eat a lot and feeding all those former country folk meant increased rural-city trade; much more city money was being infused into the rural economy than before. Not all the food, building materials, country holiday accommodations and other rural goods and services that swelled to supply the expanding Montreal market were produced in Quebec, but a lot were. What with the growing market for rural goods, and so many young people leaving the villages too, it made sense for rural people to spend some of their increased cash on labor-saving devices. Equipment to improve rural productivity—tractors, trucks, piped water, electrical appliances—thus began showing up in parishes where, in the past, there would have been neither income to buy them nor need for them. Some of the new cash also went for city-made consumer goods that in the past had been out of the question. Some went into bank deposits.

These changes had a profound effect on religious life in Quebec. Contrary to what most people believe, the Quebec religious revolution—the loss of authority of the Catholic Church—was not a cause of the city and rural changes I have mentioned, but a result of them. The local priest's word about the world and its ways was no longer the last word in settlements where almost everyone was now at least distantly acquainted with somebody who had been off to a Montreal university for a secular education; or in settlements where migrants came back from Montreal to attend weddings, funerals and family reunions; or in settlements where people now went to the movies when they got into town and at home listened to the radio, even began watching television; or in settlements where changes in the everyday economy and everyday working methods had burst the bonds of traditional ways of doing things.

One and the same force—the great growth surge of Montreal—was simultaneously undermining an old culture in the countryside and developing it into something new in the metropolis, and sending this new city-shaped culture back into the countryside.

Now we need to bring Toronto into the story. Montreal used to be the chief metropolis, the national economic center of all of Canada. It is an older city than Toronto, and until only a few years ago, it was larger. At the beginning of this century Toronto was only two-thirds the size of Montreal, and Montreal was much the more important center of finance, publishing, wholesaling, retailing, manufacturing, entertainment—everything that goes into making a city economy.

The first small and tentative shifts of finance from Montreal to Toronto began in the 1920s when Montreal banks, enamored of the blue-chip investments of the time, overlooked the financing of new mining opportunities which were then opening up in Ontario. That neglect created an opportunity for Toronto banks. The stock exchange which was set up in Toronto for trading mining shares merged with the old generalized Toronto stock exchange in 1934, and by the 1940s the volume of stocks traded in Toronto had come to exceed the volume traded in Montreal.

During the great growth surge of Montreal, from 1941 to 1971, Toronto grew at a rate that was even faster. In the first of those decades, when Montreal was growing by about 20 percent, Toronto was growing by a rate closer to 25 percent. In the next decade, when Montreal was adding a bit over 35 percent to its population, Toronto was adding about 45 percent. And from 1961 to 1971, while Montreal was growing by less than 20 percent, Toronto was growing by 30 percent. The result was that Toronto finally overtook Montreal in the late 1970s.

But even these measurements do not fully suggest what was happening economically. As an economic unit or economic force, Toronto has really been larger than Montreal for many years. This is because Toronto forms the center of a collection of satellite cities and towns, in addition to its suburbs. Those satellites contain a great range of economic activities, from steel mills to art galleries. Like many of the world's large metropolises, Toronto has been spilling out enterprises into its nearby region, causing many old and formerly small towns and little cities to grow because of the increase in jobs. In addition to that, many branch plants and other enterprises that needed a metropolitan market and a reservoir of metropolitan skills and other producers to draw upon have established themselves in Toronto's orbit, but in places where costs are lower or space more easily available.

The English call a constellation of cities and towns with this kind of economic integration a "connurbation," a term now widely adopted. Toronto's connurbation, curving around the western end of Lake Ontario, has been nicknamed the Golden Horseshoe. Hamilton, which is in the horseshoe, is larger than Calgary, a major metropolis of western Canada. Georgetown, north of Toronto, qualifies as only a small southern Ontario town, one of many in the connurbation. In New Brunswick it would be a major economic settlement.

Montreal's economic growth, on the other hand, was not enough to create a connurbation. It was contained within the city and its suburbs. That is why it is deceptive to compare population sizes of the two cities and jump to the conclusion that not until the 1970s had they become more or less equal in economic terms. Toronto supplanted Montreal as Canada's chief economic center considerably before that, probably before 1960. Whenever it happened, it was another of those things that most of us never realized had happened until much later.

Because Toronto was growing more rapidly than Montreal in the 1940s, 1950s and 1960s, and because so many of its institutions and enterprises now served the entire country, Toronto drew people not only from many other countries but from across Canada as well. The first two weeks I lived in Toronto back in the late 1960s, it seemed to me that almost everyone I encountered was a migrant from Winnipeg or New Brunswick. Had Montreal remained Canada's pre-eminent metropolis and national center, many of these Canadians would have been migrating to Montreal instead. In that case, not only would Montreal be even larger than it is today, but —and this is important—it would have remained an English Canadian metropolis. Instead it has become more and more distinctively Quebecois.

In sum, then, these two things were occurring at once: on the one hand, Montreal was growing rapidly enough and enormously enough in the decades 1941–1971 to shake up much of rural Quebec and to transform Quebec's culture too. On the other hand, Toronto and the Golden Horseshoe were growing even more rapidly. Montreal, in spite of its growth, was losing its character as the economic center of an English-speaking Canada and was simultaneously taking on its character as a regional, French-speaking metropolis.

These events, I think, are at the core of Quebec's changed and changing relationship with the rest of Canada. Things can never go back to the way they were when an English-speaking Montreal was the chief economic center of all of Canada and when life elsewhere in the province of Quebec was isolated and traditional. These changes are not merely in people's heads. They cannot be reasoned away or even voted away.

A culture can persist without its own metropolitan capital, as Quebec's did for so long. It can persist as a museum piece. But it cannot flower and thrive without a metropolis. French Quebec has its own cultural metropolis now. But to continue thriving as a cultural capital, Montreal must also thrive economically. There's the rub. As a regional Canadian city, which is what Montreal has now become, its economic future is unpromising.

To understand why this is so, we must be aware of Canada's customary view of economic life and its traditional approach to economic development. Canada exploits and exports resources, to the neglect of developing industries and services based on manufacturing or inventions requiring manufacturing. This is a profoundly colonial approach to economic life, but in Canada's case economic colonialism is not something forced upon the country. Canada prefers colonialism.

The experience of Canada has been that the largest and most quickly obtained fortunes, whether public or private, come from resources: furs, timber, apples, coal, iron, nickel, gold, copper, silver, wheat, cobalt, fish, uranium, hydroelectric power, aluminum, potash, oil, natural gas—to name some of the most influential. Societies, like individuals, are shaped by their experiences. Canada's get-rich-quick experience with resources has shaped all the country's major institutions: the national government, the provincial governments, the banks and all other financial establishments. It has shaped the way venture capital and subsidies are used, the types of development schemes contrived, and the assumptions of almost everyone in authority. These are not easy things to change.

When a single dominant approach to economic life and wealth has been pursued as consistently and as long as it has been here, the experience gets thoroughly built into how things work. It especially gets built into the uses of capital. Dazzling sums of money are available for resource exploitation and for vast construction projects associated with them, such as dams, pipelines, refineries, bulk storage and depots. When the attention of government does stray to manufacturing or innovation, as it does from time to time, the scale of effort does not adjust. Dazzling sums of money are sunk into grandiose technological schemes. To put it figuratively, if the Canadian economy were a zoo, nothing would be purchased for it except elephants.

For various reasons, many of the essays at innovation come to nothing. Some prove unworkable, like the chemical cellulose plant in the northern Quebec wilderness on which ITT lost $600 million before closing it down virtually unused, and into which the Quebec and federal governments also poured $40 million for forest equipment, roads and other support systems. Some are economically unsuccessful, like the abandoned heavy-water plant in Laprade, Quebec, which cost the two governments, federal and provincial, about $485 million. Some are plagued by bad luck and unanticipated competition, like the nuclear power system called Candu, for which the federal government has paid out $2 billion, but for which it has not been able to find the export markets that were expected to justify the investment. Sometimes endeavors that actually do appear to be succeeding are abandoned because the government's bureaucracies and political leaders become nonplused at the intelligence and patience they require, as happened when the Avro aviation design and manufacturing company in Ontario was written off after $400 million had gone into it. Not only grandiose innovations but grandiose imitations sometimes fail as well, like the oil refinery in Come-by-Chance, Newfoundland, bankrupt with $600 million in debts; the Newfoundland government holds a second mortgage of $45 million. (The holder of the first mortgage, who is proposing that the almost unused refinery be sold for scrap, is a London bank whose investment was guaranteed by the British government's Export Credits Guarantee Department.) The money that goes down the drain with each grand failure becomes a nine days' wonder.

In contrast, pitifully little capital, and even that confined mainly to Ontario, goes into initially modest innovative work. A company capable of producing an improved solenoid valve for chemical reactor plumbing systems or an efficient new type of woodburning stove is not the kind of company likely to find the modest risk capital required for such ventures. And there is almost no capital for the many small producers of bits, pieces, tools and services that the practical and economically successful development of an innovative and diverse economy requires.

All this has many consequences. One was summed up by J. J. Brown, the historian of Canadian technology, in 1967:

Canadians have made contributions to world science and technology out of all proportion to their small numbers. Some Canadian inventions made possible world industries, but we have ended up importing from England, Belgium, Italy and the United States billions of dollars worth of equipment invented here. This is our basic problem as a nation . . . If not corrected soon, it will leave us unable to compete as an industrialized nation in the modern world.

Canada is a heavy importer of humdrum and very simple consumer goods, things like hatchets, canoe paddles and waterproof match containers, and also of almost all kinds of basic industrial tools. "Orders Up, Backlogs Twice Normal for Machine Tool Industry," proclaims a December 1979 news headline in a Toronto paper. The print below proceeds to tell that the information that "this is more or less a boom year" comes from the Canadian Machine Tool Distributors Association. "Since there are only a few Canadian machine tool manufacturers," the report explains, "it is the distributors who dominate the Canadian market."

To be sure, Canada does not lack manufacturing altogether. There are uses for those imported machine tools. But of such manufacturing as the country does have, almost half is undertaken in American-owned branch plants, and—increasingly—some of the rest in other foreign-owned branch plants.

When a Canadian manufacturer does manage to get started and become successful, capital can seldom be raised for expansion of the work. This impasse is typically solved by the company's selling out to a foreign corporation. It becomes a subsidiary or a branch plant.

Most branch plants have been established, however, because of Canadian tariffs on manufactured goods. With its scanty development of producers' goods and services, Canada is in poor position to replace wide ranges of imported goods and services with its own production, as developed economies do. Canadian tariffs are imposed not to encourage indigenous economic development, but to force foreign exporters of manufactured goods to set up branch plants within Canada. This profoundly parasitic approach to "development" was largely responsible for Toronto's and Montreal's economic growth during the 1950s and 1960s; that was largely branch-plant economic growth. Branch plants in Canada must be extremely profitable because the prices charged for their goods tend to equal the price of the equivalent imports plus the high tariffs; there are few or no Canadian producers to compete. The branch plants justify their high prices by setting their own book value on components they import from other subsidiaries. And, of course, a large share of profits leaves the country.

Since there are few indigenous Canadian manufacturing enterprises available to be transplanted—as they expand—out into towns and villages where work and wages are desperately needed, the federal and provincial governments offer dazzling sums of money to foreign branch plants for that purpose too.

Naturally, all this drives Canadian economic nationalists into a fury, but even they are so unfamiliar with the fact that many modestly started enterprises go into creation of a diverse and innovative economy that they define economic colonialism narrowly and superficially. They think of it mainly as a matter of ownership, to be corrected by changes in ownership —rather than as something that can only be corrected when the economy undertakes things it now fails to *do*.

In this traditional scheme of things, Canada's regional cities also have their traditional role. They work primarily as service centers for the exploitation of resources from their hinterland. To be sure, all have some manufacturing, even the small ones like Halifax, Thunder Bay and Saskatoon and the larger ones like Winnipeg, Calgary and Edmonton, as well as the largest, Vancouver. But large or small, the regional cities of Canada do not serve as creative economic centers in their own right. They boom when the exploitation of their hinterland booms. They stagnate when the resource exploitation reaches a plateau. They decline when it declines.

This is devastating to Canadian regions where resources stop yielding more and more wealth. The passive regional cities, generating no innovations, replacing so few kinds of imports, creating so little new work, so few factories for transplanting, so few new markets themselves, cannot serve as substitute resources. Halifax, which boomed long ago when exploitation of resources in the Maritime Provinces boomed, cannot perform such services for the now impoverished Maritimes (Nova Scotia, New Brunswick and Prince Edward Island). Winnipeg, although it boomed when the wheat lands of the prairies boomed and was celebrated as the locus of the largest grain exchange in the entire world, promptly stagnated when the tasks of settling the prairie wheat lands and constructing the vast grain transportation and storage facilities had been more or less completed. Probably the currently booming Alberta oil cities of Edmonton and Calgary will stagnate in their turn—for the pattern is a consequence of Canada's curiously lopsided uses of capital and its profoundly colonial approach to economic life.

In Quebec, other cultural differences notwithstanding, the economic culture is now the same as that of English Canada. Perhaps this is because English Canada dominated Quebec economically in the past, or perhaps that fact made no difference. Whatever the reason, Quebec political leaders think, economically, exactly like most of their English-speaking counterparts. The present premier of the province, René Lévesque, an ardent Quebec nationalist and the chief proponent of sovereignty-association for Quebec, makes it clear in his writings and speeches that Quebec's economic future, as he sees it, depends on assiduous exploitation of exportable resources—and when possible, semiprocessing them before export. Claude Ryan, leader of the provincial Liberal Party and Léveque's chief political opponent, sums up Canada's economic past, present and future in these words:

> For a long time, the settlement and the cultivation of Canadian land was concentrated on a narrow band about one hundred miles wide along the United States border. But today, we are much more aware of the extraordinary wealth hidden beneath the sea on our coasts and in the vast regions of the north. Rich in minerals of all kinds, in petroleum and natural gas, in fresh-water lakes and rivers, and in forests, these areas are already the basis for a number of immense projects such as the one at James Bay, the Syncrude installations in Northern Alberta and the petroleum drilling program in the Atlantic Ocean. And this is only a beginning. These vast territories provide us with the promise of almost unlimited developments in future years and make us the envy of other countries.

The mayor of Montreal, who like Lévesque and Ryan is ardently French, has announced that the economic future of the city is rosy because it is in a good position to entice branch offices and branch plants from Europe.

I have singled out these three because of their positions, not because their faith in economic colonialism and their lack of interest in either human inventiveness or the economic possibilities of cities are unusual or extraordinary. They are very Canadian. If Montreal had not happened to be the national economic center of Canada in the past—if Halifax, say, had occupied that role or if Toronto had fallen into it much earlier than it did—Montreal would surely have been merely a passive regional city, stagnant long since. At any rate, there is little in French Canada's experience, assumptions or expectations of economic life to suggest otherwise.

Now, however, Quebec is presented with a difficulty not only unprecedented there, but unprecedented in Canada. The country has never before had a national city which lost that position and became a regional city. As a typical Canadian regional city, Montreal cannot begin to sustain the economy or the many unusual assets it has now. As it gradually subsides into its regional role, it will decline and decay, grow poor and obsolescent. No boom in resource exploitation can save it because—as a national center—it had already surpassed what even the most prosperous Canadian regional cities are capable of supporting. None of the traditional Canadian approaches can contend with this new problem.

A third of Quebec's population is concentrated in Montreal. Not only will a declining Montreal have a directly depressing effect upon that large share of the province's population, it will have a depressing effect on the province generally. The city will become a poorer market for producers in the hinterland who now depend on it. It will be a declining source of city jobs for the population at large. Its all-important cultural function in the province's life will suffer.

In sum, Montreal cannot afford to behave like other Canadian regional cities without doing great damage to the economic well-being of the Quebecois. It must instead become a creative economic center in its own right. That means it must cast up streams of new enterprises which, among them, take to producing wide ranges of goods now imported from other places, including other places in Canada, and which will generate new, city-made products and services that can be marketed outside of Montreal and Quebec as well as within; and it must become the kind of place where such enterprises can find the capital they require, and in turn generate more capital.

Yet there is probably no chance of this happening if Quebec remains a province. Canadian bankers, politicians and civil servants, captivated as they are by the siren songs of resource exploitation, ready-made branch plants, and technological grandiosities, can hardly be expected to respond to Montreal's quite different economic claims upon their attention. Beliefs and practices common to all of Canada are not apt to change simply because one city, Montreal, and one province, Quebec, so urgently need them to change.

The Quebecois themselves seem unaware of the nature of the problem which looms in their future, and given the prevailing assumptions, they may not come to understand it. But they will understand this: things are not going well.

That is why the issue of sovereignty for Quebec, now that it has been raised anew as a possibility, is not going to evaporate. Inevitably, whether or not they could do better on their own, the Quebecois are going to think they could, and many of them are going to want to try. We may expect the question of separation to be raised again and again in coming years until it is finally settled either when Canada accedes to some form of sovereignty for Quebec or when the Quebecois accept the decline of Montreal and become resigned to it and to its repercussions.

The latter seems to me unlikely. Quebec is not like the poor Maritime Provinces, which have been tied ever more tightly into Confederation by adversity and the federal government's redistributions of tax money to alleviate it. The Quebecois have a special fear: that if they themselves cannot make a success of Quebec, their long struggle will prove to have been "a sad tale told by a minority on the road to oblivion." That is how the old story of separatist sentiment in Quebec ties into the new story.

While it is quite possible that Quebec would do no better on its own than as a province of Canada, there is little reason to suppose it would do worse, and there are even some practical reasons, which I will touch on in due course, for supposing it might do better. Furthermore, as we all understand, dependence is stultifying, and sometimes the obverse is also true. That is, sometimes independence releases new kinds of effort, opens up formerly untapped funds of energy, initiative, originality and self-confidence. That has been the experience, for instance, of Norway when it broke away from Sweden at the beginning of this century.

THREE

The Secession
of Norway
from Sweden

We know little from actual experience about peaceable secessions. To be sure, Canada, Australia, New Zealand and Iceland all became independent peacefully, as did a few of the still newer nations that formerly were colonies. But those were overseas possessions of empire. With only one exception—the secession of Norway from Sweden—new nations that were former provinces or regions of another country have come to birth in violence. They have either won independence after armed insurrection, highly disruptive terrorism or civil war, or else, like the Balkans or East and West Germany, emerged as a sequel to military defeat, prostration and dismemberment by conquerors. It is difficult, if not impossible, to sort out the repercussions of such disasters from the practical consequences of the separations themselves. This is only one of many reasons that the singular case of Norway's peaceful separation is interesting.

Although the separation occurred in this century, in 1905, it seems to be little remembered, perhaps precisely because the tale lacks blood and thunder. But it does not lack conflict and struggle. The kinds of emotions that apply in the case of

Quebec, or for that matter in the cases of many violent separatist movements, were present in all their force.

Offhand, it might be supposed that the independence of Norway was easily attained, that it was a special case to begin with, because once upon a time, long ago, it had been an independent kingdom. But think of Scotland, Ulster, Wales, Burgundy, Aquitania, Catalonia, Galicia, Bavaria, Saxony, Sicily, Tuscany, Venice, the Ukraine, Latvia, Hawaii, Texas . . . one could go on and on. Nothing has been more common than the reduction of kingdoms, powerful dukedoms or independent republics to provincial status.

Norway lost its independence early in the fourteenth century to Hanseatic merchants who first nibbled away at it piecemeal by establishing rule over its ports, and then, in about 1380, allowed Denmark to take it under protection. That status became official in 1537 when the Danish king, in response to demands by his council, declared that Norway had ceased to exist as a separate realm and was henceforth part of Denmark.

So things stood until 1814, when Norway became one of the chips lost and won in the Napoleonic Wars. Great Britain and Russia promised Norway to Sweden in return for Sweden's contribution of an army corps to the fight against Napoleon and as compensation for Russia's seizure of Finland from Sweden a few years previously. Austria and Prussia agreed to ratify Norway's transfer. Denmark was out of luck because it had sided with Napoleon against Britain.

Between 1811 and 1814, at the time when the great powers were dickering over Norway, a British naval blockade severed trade and most communication between Norway and Denmark, so Norway experienced a kind of state-of-siege period of independence, lasting some three years. Up to this time, as far as history records, the Norwegians had not organized any separatist movements, but separatist schemes germinated during this three-year interval and thereafter the heady notion of independence was never lost. One is reminded of the independence movements that Britain and France found in their South Asian colonies when they returned to reclaim them after trade and most communications with them had been cut by World War II.

In Norway in 1814 there occurred by mischance a few months' hiatus between the signing by the great powers of the Treaty of Kiel, in January, which formalized the territory's transfer, and the actual assumption of Swedish rule. During this interval a self-constituted group of separatists, consisting largely of Norwegian civil servants who had held office under the Danes, rejected the Kiel treaty, proclaimed independence, chose as king a Danish prince named Christian Frederik, and arranged for an assembly representing a geographical and occupational cross section of the population to meet forthwith at a little town named Eidsvold, a few miles north of Oslo. That assembly's work was to prove vital in Norway's subsequent struggles, but apart from the success of its deliberations, everything else failed. The Swedes, when they arrived to take over their new possession, were met by a confused military resistance under the wavering leadership of the prince. Within two weeks the prince advised his quondam subjects to surrender and submit, and left the country. Norway was now part of Sweden.

In the meantime, however, most settlements had sent delegates to the Eidsvold Assembly. They did their work with incredible speed, all the more remarkable because they were there not to ratify a prepared plan of government, but to create one from scratch. In only ten days and nights they managed to debate, write and adopt a constitution. They also authorized themselves to create a national bank and national currency. The constitution provided for a monarchy and a national legislature, or parliament, to be called the Storting, meaning Great Assembly. At the time, the constitution was the most democratic in Europe. It was also so well constructed and so workable that it still serves as the Norwegian constitution today.

But grand as all this sounds, it was pitiful too. Sweden had made its own very different plans for Norway. In Swedish eyes, Norway was in effect a province. The formal arrangement was that Sweden and Norway were two kingdoms under one crown, like Scotland and England in the United Kingdom; indeed, the form had been proposed to Sweden by the British before transfer. But the actual rule was set up this way: in Stockholm, the king appointed a cabinet of Ministers for Norway composed of Norwegian career civil servants. They and their staffs lived and worked in Stockholm and served at the king's pleasure.

On matters affecting both Sweden and Norway, the Norwegian ministers joined with the Swedish ministers in one cabinet. On matters affecting only Norway, the Ministers for Norway and their staffs served as the Norwegian government. So in effect these ministerial civil servants constituted both the provincial government of Norway and a portion of the Swedish government as well. In Oslo a governor general was ensconced to represent the king and to see that the will of the king's government was executed.

In view of all this, the Storting and the Norwegian constitution would seem to have been rather in the realm of folk fantasy. Perhaps that is how the Swedish government thought of it at first: Let them have their fantasies if it amuses and occupies them. At any rate, to its great credit, Sweden neither then nor afterward banned the Storting or tried to suppress its elections, never attempted to censor its debates or interfere in its communications with the Norwegian people, and did not poison Norwegian political life with spies and secret police or corrupt it with bribes and informers.

The swift collapse of initial military resistance to Swedish rule, and the subsequent smoothness with which that rule was instituted, may account in part for Sweden's early tolerance of the Storting. But the respect which Sweden soon extended toward it and the extraordinary forbearance Sweden displayed during a later period of provocation on the part of the Storting can only be understood, I think, as an aspect of the more general nonimperialistic behavior of Sweden after the Napoleonic Wars. In striking contrast to so many nations of nineteenth-century Europe, Sweden did not embark upon seizures of empire abroad; quite as strikingly, its government did not behave imperialistically at home. The behavior was all of a piece, both at home and abroad, as nations' behavior so frequently is.

When Sweden took over Norway's rule, Norway was economically very backward. Today we would say it had a Third World economy. Most people lived by means of subsistence farming in isolated villages, or on a scanty export trade in fish and timber. By the time of Norway's separation from Sweden, ninety-one years later, it had somewhat developed. It had a few railroad lines, some decent roads, telegraph and telephone communication, and the start of a textile industry, and it was already an important ocean freight carrier and builder of ships. But it was still very poor in 1905, with little manufacturing other than that connected with the shipyards.

Thus we must visualize the entire struggle for Norwegian independence as taking place in two small and poor provincial cities, Bergen and Oslo, a few moribund ancient towns, and the scattered villages and farmsteads where most people eked out a hard existence. The pervasive poverty forced heavy emigration during much of the nineteenth century, chiefly to the United States.

Norwegians today marvel at the succession of their great men, generation after generation—farmers, foresters, craftsmen, schoolmasters, pastors and of course lawyers—who emerged from the narrow, drudging, tradition-bound life, and built independence on almost no resources except persistence and ingenuity.

During the first two years of Swedish rule the Storting managed, by persuasion, to pry loose two little fragments of Norwegian autonomy. Sweden had made what seemed to be a generous offer and probably was: the opening of military and civil appointments in both realms to people of both on equal terms. The Storting rejected the offer, and the rejection was respected by Sweden. This closed off to Norwegians the prestigious and relatively ample opportunities for public service to be found in Sweden, but of course it also meant that Swedes could not occupy government posts within Norway, and the members of the Storting evidently thought that worth the sacrifice.

The other point won was that Sweden agreed to separate its own debts from the debts incurred on behalf of Norway. In this way the Norwegians limited their own financial responsibility for Sweden, but at the same time they insisted on taking their own full share of national debt without also having the power to help determine the size of the debt, the way the money was raised, what the money was to be used for, or how the taxes to support interest on the debt were to be levied.

The Norwegians were also determined to use their own central bank and their own currency which that hasty meeting of the constitutional assembly had authorized, and amazingly enough they did so, although with the greatest difficulty. They issued bank notes on a silver standard, but since they could not raise the needed amount of silver, the currency was extremely unstable until 1842. (Between then and 1875 it worked very well. Then Sweden tied it to the Swedish krona and established a mutual gold standard. After independence, Norway again adopted an independent currency, which it still has.)

Thus two persistent themes were set by the Norwegians from the very beginning of their struggle for independence, which thereafter ran through the entire effort. One theme was their fearlessness, poor though they were, in taking financial responsibility for their own affairs, indeed their positive eagerness to do so. The other was their strategy of seeking and grasping whatever bit, piece or symbol of independence they could find, no matter how irrational it might be, given their subordinate status.

They did not win another of those fragments until 1821, when they got themselves a flag. It was not the national flag which they would have liked; a national flag was denied them on grounds that Sweden's flag was their flag too. Nevertheless, they got permission to use this flag of theirs on merchant ships as Norway's commercial emblem in northern waters. Years later they won the right to use the trade flag on all the oceans. So it went in the Storting, symbol or substance, push, push, push over the years, always for a little bit more. In 1837 they won another bit of financial responsibility: the right of local taxpayers to govern local expenditures for purely local matters.

Not all the ideas came from the Storting. A young poet named Henrik Wergeland conceived the idea, in 1824, of an annual celebration on May 17, the date of the adoption of the constitution. The idea caught on and the day became, as it still remains, a great Norwegian national holiday. Wergeland's father, a clergyman, had not only been a delegate to the Eidsvold Assembly but was also the pastor of Eidsvold, where the poet was born and brought up; he had been a child of six at the time of the assembly, and what had been done there remained his pride and his passion. Wergeland was one of those improbably romantic, willful, bohemian geniuses who have so often helped give soul and fire to freedom movements. Young always in people's memory because he was short-lived, he was, besides being a poet, a standard-bearer for every democratic cause he learned of, whether in Norway or anywhere else, and a tireless expositor of politics and economics, "as though Shelley had also been Cobbett," according to an English historian. On the strength of his shorter lyrical works, Norwegians consider him the greatest poet their country has produced. But perhaps his most extraordinary outpouring was a 720-page poem written when he was twenty-two, called nothing less than *Creation, Man and Messiah.* It is not read much today, but it evidently had an electrifying effect at the time. A later Norwegian poet said of him, "He willed a union of workman and king, law-breaker and law-maker, the wise man and the fool. And Norway's woods and mines and factories, her ploughlands, fisheries and shipping—right down to the beasts and the birds, he included them all."

A national holiday, an almost-flag, a few rather disjointed bits of financial autonomy—this was about the sum of independence Norway had won during the first half of the period when it was ruled by Sweden. After forty-five years, the career civil servants still governed aloofly in Stockholm, their orders transmitted through the governor general. The conflict, though earnest enough, had remained exceedingly tame. But beginning in 1859, all this changed when the Storting turned balky and set in motion the train of events that was to culminate, finally, in secession.

That year the Storting rejected two measures which had been adopted in Stockholm. One of the changes would have made decisions by law courts in either Sweden or Norway binding in both; the other would have established a joint customs union. At the time—although not later—the issue of a customs union had little practical meaning because the Norwegian ministers in Stockholm decided such questions as tariffs anyhow and did what Sweden wanted. Sweden acceded to the Storting's wishes on both these matters.

But at the same time that the Storting rejected the two measures for closer union and made the rejections stick, it also put forward a proposal of its own which was to have far-reaching consequences—a proposal that Sweden abolish the post of governor general. That proposal, and Sweden's refusal to accept it, signaled the end of tame and gentle conflict and inaugurated forty-six years of recurrent and ever more serious political crises and acrimony.

The question arises, of course, why the change in temper occurred at all, and, moreover, occurred abruptly and unexpectedly. No particular event of any sort precipitated the new Norwegian intransigence. It seems probable that an aggregation of economic and cultural changes, along with the development in Norway of a counterindependence movement, all of which had gradually been gathering force, ignited the Storting or combined to stiffen both its resistance and its aggressiveness.

Norway had recently discovered that in at least one economic field it not only could outdo Sweden but could compete successfully with the whole world. Ten years earlier, in 1849, the British had repealed their Navigation Acts, throwing open the trade of the whole British Empire to free competition among freight carriers. Many other countries, starting with Holland, soon imitated Britain. Traditionally, Norway's exports had been timber and fish, and traditionally, these exports had been carried in Norwegian ships. For some time, gradually and slowly as opportunities arose, Norwegian shipowners had added to this work the activity of carrying cargo for non-Norwegian shippers. Thus, at the time of the Navigation Acts repeal they were in a position to seize the new and much multiplied opportunities to be opened. They anxiously tracked the British measure as it made its way through Parliament, and a Norwegian ship was the first to inaugurate the new era; it was unloading Canadian timber at the London docks within a week after free competition was introduced. By 1859, cargo-carrying was well on its way to becoming the Norwegians' major export work and the largest source of employment for Norwegian men apart from subsistence farming.

The confidence and pride created by this first important economic success were being reinforced by cultural excitements and successes. The Norwegians had lacked, or thought they had lacked, a language of their own. The language of the pulpit, the press, the schools, the government, the capital city, all educated people wherever they lived in Norway, and many who were uneducated too, was Danish, owing to the centuries-long Danish occupation and rule. The Norwegians pronounced the Danish in a way of their own (nowadays it is called Dano-Norwegian).

Actually there was another language, or rather, a great many different dialects of another language. Collectively the vernacular might be thought of as "Norwegian," but practically speaking, there was no definitive or nationally useful Norwegian language because the dialects, although linguistically closely related, were in some cases mutually incomprehensible. Northern and southern Norwegians in particular were at a loss to understand one another's mother tongues. All the dialects were also linguistically related, although more distantly, to Danish. The situation was rather as if Norman

French had persisted as the language of London and of all official and educated communication in the realm of England, while in the English countryside people spoke mutually incomprehensible dialects of "English."

Wergeland, ardent nationalist though he was, had written his poetry, essays and polemics in Danish. There was nothing else for him to write in. The necessity had galled him, and he had wistfully thrown out the idea that Danish ought somehow to be "Norwegianized."

Not only did the Norwegians have no language of their own, they had produced hardly any literature of their own since the dim and remote times of the Old Norse sagas. So they assumed that they had no culture of their own as that word is usually understood. However, in the 1830s two young Norwegian students, Jörgen Moe and Peter Christen Asbjörnsen, traveled among remote farmsteads and villages, and listened. In the 1840s they began publishing what they had heard—stories of loutish and bombastic giants, brutal and disgusting trolls, shrewd and industrious dwarfs, and wise, wily maidens. Today one can find the favorites, usually credited to Moe and Asbjörnsen, in many English anthologies of fairy and folk tales.

Publication created a sensation in Oslo. The stories themselves were a revelation. Their originality, fantasy and beauty —and their view of life—revealed a side of the national character Norwegians themselves had hardly appreciated. But the real bombshell was the language. The authors incorporated into the Danish as much native Norwegian vocabulary and idiom as they could while at the same time keeping the work understandable to city readers. Asbjörnsen, besides being co-editor, did the publishing (to earn his living he was a professional forester), and each time he brought out a new edition he and Moe enriched the language brew, rendering the indigenous elements still more numerous and prominent. By the time the definitive edition was published, in 1851, not only had a new literary style been created, based upon preference for selecting words of Norwegian origin, but also a new and practical method for deliberately developing a language. Others took up the method, and even today the intentional and conscious evolution of the language continues. Norwegian friends tell me new words and turns of speech are still being rediscovered and incorporated, and that people still find the process fun and exciting. The language that was developing in this fashion was to be recognized in the 1890s, under the name *nynorsk* (neo-Norwegian), as a second official language, making Norway bilingual, which it still is.

Moe, who was a poet as well as co-editor of the folk tales, was appointed Reader in Folklore at Oslo University in 1849, probably the first such appointment in the world. A few years later the first realistic Norwegian novel was published. The author, Camilla Collett, was a sister of the poet Wergeland. This book, too, which was written in proper Danish, created a sensation. Called *The County Governor's Daughters,* it attacked the traditional upbringing of girls and paved the way for the women's emancipation movement which was to get under way in Norway in the 1870s.

Along with folklore and fiction came history. Starting in 1852, Norway's leading historian, P. A. Munch, began publishing the six volumes of his *History of the Norwegian People,* and at the same time led the preservationists in a battle over whether the ruins of the ancient cathedral in Trondheim should be torn down as an "improvement" or be saved. Munch used this struggle as an opportunity to educate his countrymen in the achievements and civilization of medieval

Norway. The preservationists not only won but went on to start a movement for restoration of the ruins, a vast and ambitious task that even now is still in process.

Thus, in the middle of the nineteenth century, Norwegians were finding that they had a history in which it was possible for them to take pride, a language that it was possible to use and enjoy, and the beginnings of a literature of their own. The excitement all this generated was a bit exaggerated, if anything, then and later. According to an English historian of modern Norway, "anything done by a Norwegian in the arts and sciences, commerce and even sport had always to be vociferously acclaimed as the triumph of a specifically Norwegian culture . . ."

But alongside the cultural and nationalist ferment, another movement had been arising which ran counter to Norway's aspirations for independence. Called Scandinavianization, the object of that movement was the unification of Denmark, Norway and Sweden into a single nation.

Unifications and territorial expansion were in the air everywhere. The German principalities were uniting into the North German Federation, which became the German Empire. Russia was in the process of unifying Siberia under the rule of the czar. The United States, expanding westward to the Pacific, had engulfed territories seized in the Mexican War and was on the threshold of the Civil War, which so decisively would settle the issue of American unity. In Canada the time was approaching for Confederation under the British North America Act, and in Italy schemes for unification were beginning to germinate. Austria and Hungary were sealing the union that was to hold their empire together for another half-century. In the wake of the Sepoy Mutiny, Britain was joining together under the British raj a bewildering variety of Indian states and principalities; and at the same moment French administrators of what is now Vietnam were concluding that Cambodia, too, must be united into their Indochinese holdings for protection of their position. Everywhere, at home and abroad, great powers and would-be great powers were getting their ducks in a row: readying themselves for the rivalries and slaughters of our own century.

As for Scandinavianization, one of its many European enthusiasts, Louis Napoleon of France, said in 1856, "The North must become one unit, one strong power, a counterweight both to Russia and to Germany."

At the time, of course, unification was widely thought of as progress in the art of government, and aggrandizement as the way to spread civilization. In Scandinavia, as elsewhere, political unification appealed strongly to those who conceived of it as a means of transcending differences and erasing conflicts in favor of cooperation, harmony and mutual aid. The chief stronghold of the Scandinavian movement for unification was in the universities. The importance of this lay in the fact that the students, who were a tiny minority of youth at the time, could be expected in due course to make up the civil services and other educated leadership of Sweden, Norway and Denmark. The Swedish king favored the movement, as did many of the larger landholders in all three countries. Throughout the 1850s and early 1860s, when the movement was at its height, its success appeared all but inevitable.

But when Germany went to war against Denmark in 1864 to seize the province of Schleswig-Holstein, the Scandinavian movement was abruptly put to the test. Those in Norway who favored it insisted that Norwegians must enlist on Denmark's side; Norwegians overwhelmingly refused to do any such thing. The whole movement collapsed, never to rise again. Among those who were outraged was Ibsen, an idealistic and dedicated proponent of Scandinavianization. Some say his disillusionment and anger at what he considered his fellow Norwegians' blindness, and his bitterness at the movement's collapse because of their provincialism, as he saw it, were among the reasons he then exiled himself from his country.

The movement, however, had long and lingering consequences in Norway after its collapse. It continued to divide the population, with those who had favored Scandinavianization tending to lean toward closer union with Sweden, against those who preferred greater Norwegian autonomy.

Now let us get back to the Storting, which was where the battle was to be waged, and which we left in 1859 when the Storting's proposal to abolish the governor general was turned down by Sweden. The Swedish government had remained placatory and patient with the cantankerous Norwegians. When the Storting chose to make an issue of the governor-generalship, immediately after rejecting Sweden's plans for customs and legal union, the king and his advisers remained patient, even sympathetic. They were prepared to accede to the Storting's request and abolish the governor general's post.

But when word of this intention became known, an angry wave of Swedish public opinion prevented the government from proceeding. One can understand this Swedish reaction. After all, Sweden had consistently behaved decently toward Norway within the framework of the fact that Norway was a Swedish possession. Yet the Norwegians obdurately refused to take pleasure or pride in their association with Sweden. They would not even meet the Swedes halfway, and made no bones about it. Concessions, it seemed, were always being made by Sweden, never by Norway.

Instead of backing off in the face of this evidence of Swedish hostility, the Storting obstinately continued to press the issue of the governor-generalship. Session after session it passed the same resolution over and over again, and over again presented it to the king. Finally, after fourteen years of what must have come to seem to Sweden a case of monomania, Norway got its way.

In place of the governor-generalship, with its connotations of colonial rule, Sweden created a new office, Minister of State for Norway. The position was analagous to that of prime minister in the sense that the new official was the highest-ranking Norwegian minister, but unlike a prime minister under a parliamentary system he was appointed in Stockholm and was still responsible to the government there. The immediate gain for Norway was symbolic: the implication that the center of authority had moved from Stockholm to Oslo.

But this change was only the first step in a more ambitious scheme the Storting's leadership had in mind—attainment of responsible government under a true parliamentary system. Now that Norway had a quasi prime minister, the Storting passed a bill demanding that the Ministers for Norway, those aloof civil servants in Stockholm, come to Oslo and sit in the Storting as ministers would do under a parliamentary system, and become responsible to the Storting. The bill outraged Swedish public opinion again, and it was promptly vetoed in Sweden. Hostility between the two peoples mounted. These tensions were to increase to the point where, during the next thirty years, until separation, on at least three occasions it appeared that either country might take up arms against the other.

In the Storting itself a situation now existed that was tailor-made for conflict and crisis. The membership had formed into two political parties. The larger, representing separatist sentiment, was led by Johan Sverdrup, a brilliantly resourceful lawyer, chief strategist of the scheme for attaining responsible government. This faction, although it constituted a majority, held no de facto power. The minority party, representing the unionists, was formally in charge because its leader was the appointed quasi prime minister in whom authority resided. In addition, the government civil service—which exerted most of the real power—was composed of unionists. In election after election the separatists were returned to the Storting with decisive majorities, yet in effect remained the minority party.

Their one effective form of strength was their ability to win issues put to a vote in the Storting, and they proceeded to use this asset with rather breath-taking boldness. What they did was vote to amend the Norwegian constitution in a way that specifically required the Ministers for Norway to come sit in the Storting, respond to its questions and act under its direction. Tactically, this was not a mere repetition of the previous resolution asking the same thing; it was a constitutional amendment. Naturally, the amendment was vetoed in Sweden. But the Storting then proceeded to pass it twice more, each time after elections that returned larger and larger separatist majorities, and to announce—after the third passage, in 1880—that it was now law regardless of vetoes because it fulfilled the Norwegian constitution's own provisions for amendment. Thereupon the Storting ordered the Ministers for Norway to obey the constitution and submit to the Storting. Of course they refused.

A four-year legal wrangle of stupendous complexity followed. Overruling a decision of the Rigsret (Supreme Court of Norway) and an opinion from the law faculty of the University of Oslo, the Storting then proceeded to impeach the ministers, convict them, levy fines against them and declare their offices forfeit and vacant. Through all this, tempers in Sweden rose and so did tempers in Norway. This was one of the occasions when violence appeared probable. The Norwegians feared a royal military coup, which had been rumored. Volunteer rifle clubs began organizing in Norway to resist such a takeover.

The Swedish government and king, who throughout the crisis had continued to speak in voices of moderation and to do their best to calm down the hotheads on both sides, now were faced with only two choices: either Sweden must enforce its rule over Norway by military means, which clearly meant civil war, or else it must accede to the Storting's demand for responsible government.

Sweden chose the peaceful course. The king asked Sverdrup to form a cabinet. Government of Norway by Norway, the grand and pitiful public fantasy of Eidsvold, seventy years before, had finally become reality.

The uses to which the Storting put its new powers were exemplary from a democratic point of view. It concerned itself with such things as introducing the jury system for criminal cases, improving the school system, providing for locally elected school boards, extending suffrage. More ominously, it reorganized the Norwegian army on a more democratic basis. From this point on, the Storting could count on the army.

Things calmed down for a few years. The unionists accepted responsible government as a fact of life and even won an election or two because of splits in the separatist party over personalities and strategies. But beginning in 1888, the conflict flared up anew, this time shifting to economic issues. Norway, in spite of its success with shipping and shipbuilding was still, on the whole, terribly poor and the 1880s were proving lean years indeed. Emigration was the only means through which many young Norwegians could find a tolerable livelihood of any sort; in some years during this decade, in which emigration reached its high tide, net population actually dropped for that reason. Norway's basic economic problem at this time was its underdeveloped domestic economy. It simply did not produce amply or diversely for its own people, and what it did not produce for itself it obviously had to import or else go without; that included most kinds of manufactured goods. Thus it was exceedingly vulnerable to the least weakening in its export trade.

At the time Sweden, too, was relatively underdeveloped economically, although it had become better equipped industrially than Norway was. To promote and encourage the development of indigenous industry, the Swedish government in 1888 adopted a policy of very high tariffs, and it directed those tariffs quite as much against Norwegian imports as against those of other nations. Perhaps there was some element of satisfaction in this move, some glee in retaliating against Norway for having once rejected customs union and for having won the great tussle over responsible government. Sweden was the chief export customer for the very few kinds of manufactured goods that Norway did produce, chiefly cloth being made by an incipient modern textile industry centering around Bergen. That market was being abruptly cut off. The Norwegians, with an economy already so close to the bone, felt as if the bone itself were being gnawed.

The only way Norway could compensate for losses of export trade with Sweden was to increase its exports elsewhere, and the only swift and practical way of doing that was to find more customers abroad for the work of the Norwegian merchant fleet. But here Sweden had Norway in a bind.

As far as foreign affairs were concerned, Norway was still a part of Sweden. Norway had no consular representation of its own; instead, it contributed toward support of a joint consular service. Norwegians had long resented the disadvantages of this arrangement, disadvantages which were symbolized by the plight of a poor Norwegian seaman in difficulties in a foreign port, given no understanding and short shrift by an aristocratic Swedish consul. Now, when Norway needed rapid and effective consular aid to find, develop and service new markets for Norwegian cargo shipping, Swedish consuls were not that interested in hustling for Norway. The gap between what Norway needed and what it was getting soon became so serious economically that the Storting, in 1892, voted to withhold its consular contributions to the Stockholm government and unilaterally establish a service of its own.

The king vetoed the measure. But since he was a constitutional monarch of the two countries, his veto had to be countersigned by the ministers of the Norwegian government. In the past, that requirement had presented no problem, but now the ministers were men chosen by the Storting and responsible to it. They refused to sign. This was a new kind of impasse. The king dissolved the government and appointed a new cabinet, its members drawn from the minority unionist party. But the Storting refused to countenance this arrangement, and the new government could not govern a Storting and a people who would not be governed by it. Its attempts to rule were a shambles. In Sweden public opinion against Norway was again rising alarmingly, and again there were rumors of war.

Now it was the Norwegians' turn to realize they had only two choices: either they could pay up their contribution and try to negotiate more attention to their needs or else they could make war to try to establish complete independence. The reason complete independence was the only alternative to the status quo was that Norway had already made a tentative stab at establishing its own consuls in Germany, but Germany had refused to recognize them because its diplomatic relations were with Sweden, not Norway. The response, Norwegians knew, would be the same in all other countries.

Norway chose the peaceful course. It paid up and negotiated. But no agreement could be reached, and the talks eventually broke down entirely. Tempers in both countries grew uglier. The Norwegians embarked on a strong rearmament program and strengthened fortifications along their border. Again, war looked imminent.

This time it was Sweden's turn to back off. It did so by suggesting a compromise permitting separate consular services under a single diplomatic staff. On this basis, negotiations began again, but in reality the Swedish position against Norway was hardening and the talks got nowhere. As frustration in Norway mounted, the issue of the consuls escalated in almost everyone's mind there into the issue of complete independence. Even the party of the unionists, who felt betrayed by the Swedish negotiators, was now ready to embrace secession.

The Storting organized itself into a coalition government representing both parties, and chose as prime minister Christian Michelsen, a Bergen lawyer and shipowner. Plebiscites were called in Norway, great demonstrations were mounted, the country was in an uproar, and in the spring of 1905 the Storting unanimously passed a bill demanding thoroughly separate consular services with the implication that the issue was no longer negotiable.

The form the crisis took this time was a curious legalistic deadlock, a kind of Gordian knot. When the king vetoed the Storting's bill, the ministers—as expected—refused to countersign his veto and resigned. All that was somewhat familiar. But this time the king refused to accept the resignations because that move had resulted in such a mess the previous time it was employed. In refusing, he said, "No other cabinet can now be formed."

The words of the king meant one thing in Sweden—that Norway must now knuckle under—but in Norway they were chosen to mean something different. The prime minister, Michelsen, who was much admired among his countrymen for his nimble mind and efficiency, quick-wittedly used the king's remark to mean that the king himself had dissolved the union between Norway and Sweden, and proceeded deftly to slice through the tangle in which affairs had been left. His argument was that the king could exercise his royal functions only constitutionally, which was true, and that since this meant that he could exercise them only through a cabinet, he himself—by announcing that none could be formed—had declared he could no longer rule Norway and so had dissolved the union himself. This went over as a great idea in the Storting. It promptly passed a resolution, on June 7, 1905, announcing that Norway's union with Sweden was at an end and then proceeded to act as the government of a fully sovereign state.

Of course, that did not quite end the matter. As may be supposed, a tense time followed. The Swedish Riksdag (Parliament) refused to admit that the union had been dissolved and countermanded what the Storting had done. But once again, Sweden recognized that the question was one of war or peace. Denmark, Russia and France all urged Sweden to show moderation, and Sweden proceeded to resolve matters in this fashion: if the Norwegians would agree to meet certain conditions, then Sweden would be willing to negotiate for dissolution. The chief conditions were that Norway should dismantle its border forts, that a military neutral zone should be created along the southern frontier between Norway and Sweden, and that Norway must hold a referendum to see whether its people actually did want dissolution.

The conditions were agreeable to Norway. Indeed, the government had already arranged for a referendum to take place in August. It produced a huge outpouring of votes, overwhelmingly in favor of independence, and negotiations between the two governments were promptly started. They were complex and difficult, but now Sweden had accepted the fact that Norway had seceded; and Norway, for its part, recognized that it was being dealt with in good faith. In this anticlimactic atmosphere the arrangements moved so rapidly and were accepted in both countries so readily that before the year was out, all had been settled.

The Norwegians invited Carl, grandson of the king of Denmark and son-in-law of the king of England, to be their constitutional monarch. He took the medieval name of Haakon, an inspiration suggested by one of the poet Wergeland's apostrophes to Norway, poured out so many years before: "With what joy thy towers would shine, saw they Haakon's age again." He was crowned in Trondheim Cathedral, saved from destruction so many years before by Munch. Everybody's labor, whether for symbol or substance, was bearing fruit. "The feelings of relief and of enhanced self-respect," a historian has written, "were comparable to those which other peoples associate with the winning of a major war. It would hardly be too much to say that many Norwegians thought of the whole of their history since 1319 as a wandering in the wilderness from which they had now emerged into the Promised Land."

It is difficult to say whether the outcome did greater honor to Sweden or to Norway. It seems to me that it did honor not only to both but also to civilization.

The separation, as it turned out, has harmed neither country. On the contrary, it probably helped them both, economically as well as politically. The conflict itself, which could only have grown uglier and more dangerous, was disposed of. Sweden was certainly better off economically in the years to follow than it would have been if it had had to carry on its back a poverty-stricken province, as might well have been the case.

Norway had its ups and downs. Things seemed to start out well economically after independence, with the beginnings of the development of electric-power, chemical and metallurgical industries. But no sooner did Norway's economy begin to blossom noticeably than the government became too ambitious in its social programs, which soon outran the economy's capacity to pay for them. In an attempt to support them anyhow, the government took to printing money exuberantly and a terrible inflation followed, much intensifying the general inflation which Norway, like all Europe, experienced during World War I. The exaggerated Norwegian inflation raged from 1916 to 1920. The government then retrenched, and by 1928 the effects had been overcome. But after three brief years of prosperity and stability, the world-wide depression engulfed Norway. Norway's recovery, however, began earlier than that of most countries. By 1934 the economy was markedly improved, and Norway's economic development has been both rapid and many-sided since. In the course of developing their economy, the Norwegians have displayed an inventiveness and verve that it is hard to imagine they could have exercised had they and their government been preoccupied instead with bitter political grievances and associated economic frustrations.

Today Sweden and Norway are each other's best customers. The two cooperate as equals in many fields. They have joint customs inspections, have abolished passport requirements for each other's citizens, have coordinated their university standards and their social insurance arrangements, have established a common labor market, and they engage in various joint scientific projects and some joint industrial ventures. But when they want to differ, they do. For instance, Sweden, like Denmark, has become a member of the European Economic Community, but Norway has not. Its government favored membership, but its people turned it down in a referendum.

Here in Toronto, where I live, in two different office buildings about a mile apart, are to be found two trade commissions, one Norwegian, one Swedish. To me, the two establishments seem more than busy, competently run commercial offices, staffed by cheerful, helpful people. To me, they seem the concrete evidence of a miracle—a secession achieved without armed rebellion, without terrorism, without the military defeat of a former ruler.

In the Swedish office I recently asked one of the civil servants how Swedes really feel toward Norwegians today: "Do they harbor feelings of resentment about the secession?" He looked shocked at the idea. "Of course not," he said. "We make jokes—" and he blushed. "The same jokes you tell in Canada about Newfies.* But they are good neighbors, good customers, our best, and they have made a fine country for themselves." Then he added reflectively, "We wanted them to like being with us, but . . ." and he shook his head.

There are many obvious differences between Quebec and Norway and between Canada and Sweden. For instance, Quebec is much richer and better developed economically than Norway was at the time when Norwegian sovereignty hung in the balance. Quebec got responsible government earlier than Norway, and more easily. Quebec's population is larger than Norway's; and Canada's—even without Quebec—is much larger than Sweden's.

But there are many similarities too. Quebec, for many years, has been trying to take more of its affairs into its own hands. These moves, as in Norway, jumble symbols with substance; demands for responsibility with claims to cultural equality; economic concerns with political preoccupations. An intricate,

*Naïve Newfoundlanders.

pervasive drive is at work in Quebec, as it was in Norway. The slogan of Quebec's quiet revolution, "Masters in our own house," was not invoked in Norway, as far as I know; yet that is clearly what the Norwegian struggle was all about.

Canada, for its part, is similar to Sweden in its recoil against the idea of civil war or use of military force to keep Quebec in its place. Canadians are similar to Swedes in not wanting a separation, and in wanting the people of Quebec to take pride in being Canadian. They are also like Swedes in being impatient with Quebec's never-ending train of grievances and in being hostile toward Quebec's never-ending train of demands. But the government in Ottawa, like the government in Stockholm, is a voice of moderation in comparison with the anger and hostility against Quebec vented in such places as letters-to-the-editor columns, many newspaper editorials, or on the part of some of the provincial governments. If Quebec does continue a course of moving toward independence, I have an unshakable feeling that Canada's behavior, like Sweden's, will do honor to civilization.

FOUR

National Size and Economic Development

Norway and Sweden have highly developed economies. While both have their problems, as things go in this world they are extremely well off. They produce amply and diversely for their own people's and producers' needs, as well as for export. They are efficient and innovative, and the wide ranges of their enterprises afford their peoples wide ranges of jobs and opportunities.

Norway with its four million people, Sweden with slightly more than eight million, have small populations compared to Canada, which has almost twenty-four million people. If Quebec should separate, it would have a national population half again as large as Norway's. Without Quebec, Canada's national population would still be more then twice Sweden's.

Yet the thought of Quebec becoming a small independent country, and of Canada becoming smaller than it is now, strikes many Canadians as alarming because they think Canada is already economically handicapped by having a "small" population. Consider, for example, this analysis:

Canada has the smallest domestic market of any major industrialized nation. That market, in addition, is more deeply penetrated by import goods than any of the other industrialized nations.

These factors make it difficult for Canadian manufacturers to achieve sufficient scale of operation to support world scale technology, to permit adequate research and development activities, or to compete effectively in world markets.

The argument comes from a fact sheet, as it is called, put out by the government of Ontario. But it could just as well have been plucked from any of hundreds of speeches, reports or panel sessions. It is also the sort of statement that constantly crops up in Canadian newspapers, either in their reports of what the experts say or as parenthetical explanation of Canadian deficiencies in this, that and the other field of technology, service or manufacturing.

The argument sounds plausible because it is true that Canadian manufacturing is skimpy, its nature is imitative, and so much of it was actually developed in America and is now carried on in American branch plants. The United States has a domestic market almost ten times the size of Canada's. If we make those observations and then stop thinking, we do indeed seem to have an economic argument that bigger is better. But if we lift our eyes from Canada and the United States, we wonder. Canada's domestic market is huge in comparison not only with that of Norway, Sweden, Denmark or Finland, but also with Switzerland, Belgium or the Netherlands. Small size does not seem to have handicapped the economy of those countries, as Canadians assume it to have handicapped theirs. Nor does the existence of the European Common Market account for the anomaly. After all, Norway and Switzerland are not even members, and some of the others have become members so recently that this cannot begin to account for their development. Also, many very large nations have severely underdeveloped economies and pervasive poverty. India, China and Nigeria are obvious examples.

If we were to look at Norway and Sweden in relation to the Soviet Union, or if we were to compare the Netherlands or Switzerland with much more populous Spain or Britain, and if we were to reason that qualitative differences between these various nations' economies were caused by the differing sizes of their domestic markets, we would have to come to exactly the opposite conclusion from that endorsed by the Ontario fact sheet I quoted. We would have to deduce that a small domestic market is an important asset, and a large domestic market a severe handicap.

Of course that is not true either. Small countries can have miserable economies. Many do. Small Central American, Caribbean, South American and African countries afford examples; Portugal and Albania are obvious instances in Europe. It is as misleading to jump to the conclusion that small is beautiful as it is to assume that big is better. What a look at the real world does tell us is that other things must be much more important to the development of an economy than the size of the domestic market—or at any rate, than the size of a country's population.

In relation to the United States, Canada has a colonial economy. It sells the United States, its chief trading partner, raw and semiprocessed materials, and in return buys chiefly manufactured goods. But in relation to Norway, which is so small, Canada also has a colonial economy. We send Norway nickel ores and ore concentrates. Norway sends back nickel anodes, cathodes, ingots and rods, more than $100 million worth in 1979. Taken alone, the nickel trade might reflect nothing more than the ways in which multinational corporations choose to rationalize their production, since this particular trade is controlled by Falconbridge Nickel, a corporation with mines in Canada and processing works in Norway. However, that trade happens to be consistent with a general trading pattern that cannot be explained away as the outcome of big decisions on the part of a few big producers.

Only 15 percent of what we in Canada send to Norway is processed and manufactured goods, but half of what Norway sends us is processed and manufactured. Some of those goods are similar in kind. That is, Norway sends us thermometers, we send Norway thermostats; we trade each other mining equipment, sound amplifiers, semiconductors, carpets, mittens, toys, hockey equipment and quite a few other things. But significantly, Norway sends us about 30 percent more *kinds* of manufactured and processed items than we send Norway. Furthermore, of the twelve chief items each country trades with the other, only three of Canada's are manufactured goods, while six of Norway's are.

Norway's biggest exports to Canada include farm machinery, commercial fishing equipment and skis. Canada is a much bigger and much more important farming country than Norway. One of our largest exports to Norway is wheat—and one of our largest imports from Norway is farm machinery. That is a classic colonial pattern if there ever was one.

Canada also has a big domestic market for commercial fishing equipment and skis. The ski imports have become so large that Canada recently put a new tariff on skis. The tariff is so high that it has compelled (as was its object) a Norwegian company to build a branch plant in Canada—in Ontario, as it happens—from which it is now prepared to supply about 100,000 pairs of skis annually, to the same market, if we were to believe the government of Ontario, that is too small to be economic for Canadian manufacturers.

As for what the statement I quoted calls "world scale technology" and "adequate research and development activities," Norway and its manufacturers do fine. Glancing through the news items in the Export Council of Norway's 1979 Annual, I find, for instance, that a Norwegian company is exporting to the United States and to Sweden a computer-controlled system for maintaining a vessel in exact position without need for anchors; another is building and equipping five fertilizer factories for the Soviet Union; another is supplying the Soviet Union with a factory to produce pipes and tanks of glass fiber reinforced polyester; another is selling China underwater seismic equipment for geophysical survey work; the Annual contains dozens more of such items.

Norway is energy-rich, like Canada, but is less complacent about its wealth of oil and water power. Having reached a point at which a choice had become advisable between continuing to flood valleys for expansion of hydroelectric power or preserving valleys, timberlands and wilderness, Norway drew a line. It favors preservation. Consequently, Norwegian enterprises, in some cases in cooperation with the government, have for some years now been experimenting seriously with tidal, wind and solar power, with new applications for heat pumps, and with new power applications for charcoal and wood chips. Some of this work in due course will likely emerge as "world scale technology." Norway is a pioneer at ocean fishfarming; this takes place in some of the country's fjords, which are much like British Columbia's fjords.

Much of Norway's manufacturing for its own consumers is in small-scale enterprises, but that does not mean the manufacturing is either uneconomic or backward. In 1970, which is the last year for which I have figures, Norway had almost 600 furniture factories, only 35 of which employed more than fifty persons. Yet far from needing economic protection, Norway's furniture industry was competing internationally, with great success. Norway exports furniture to Canada. In time, perhaps, we in Canada will be importing Norwegian houses. At any rate, by 1970 some 230 different Norwegian firms were manufacturing prefabricated houses, mostly for summer or winter vacation use. Thus far that production is still only for Norway's small domestic market; yet that is how the furniture manufacturing began, as well as the manufacturing of skis, tents, hiking and camping clothing, knives and many other consumer goods that have become valuable Norwegian exports, purchased and prized by consumers in many countries other than Canada.

Norway's small domestic market is obviously economically potent, while Canada's much bigger domestic market is, equally obviously, impotent. What is responsible for that difference? We can get a clue by going back to the time when Norway and one part of Canada had almost identical economies.

Today the poorest part of Canada is the Atlantic provinces, among them Nova Scotia. A century and a half ago, both Nova Scotia's and Norway's chief exports were fish and timber, while in both places most people eked out a living by subsistence farming. At first the Nova Scotian fish and timber exports were carried by British and American fleets, but early in the nineteenth century Nova Scotians began building ships of their own for their export trading, just as Norwegians had done. And, again like Norwegian shippers, Nova Scotia's shipowners branched out in their work. They began carrying cargo for other countries. The work of shipping itself, in its own right, had become export work for Nova Scotia. And just as happened in Norway, when the work of the ships expanded, the work of the shipyards expanded too. By the mid-nineteenth century the clipper ships of Nova Scotia were to be found in all the oceans, helping to carry the commerce of the world. The shipyards of Nova Scotia came to employ about three thousand workmen, which may not seem like much today, but this represented a considerable force of skilled specialists, an appreciable industry, in a scanty population of farmers, fishermen and woodsmen, just as Norway's shipbuilders were a considerable force of specialists, in an appreciable industry for its time and place. But just about a century ago, these twin economies took sharply different directions. In Norway, shipbuilding started making the transition from wood to steel, and from sail to steam. But in Nova Scotia that transition was never made.

Coal and iron had been discovered in Nova Scotia. Never was there an economy in an inherently better position to make a significant transition in its most important industry than Nova Scotia's economy just then. But the chance was thrown away. Money could be made more rapidly in Nova Scotia by exporting the newly discovered coal and iron than by converting shipbuilding. The question that leaps to mind is, of course, Why not do both? The answer, apparently, is that the capitalists of the place and time were uninterested in doing both. One can see why. Exploiting and exporting resources, then as today, brought quick and large returns, and had other advantages, too. What had to be financed were just a few, big, relatively simple projects. Converting shipbuilding carried the disadvantage of financing many, and more various, and inherently more innovative projects, hence more risk. At any rate, the money and the efforts went into the get-rich-quick resource work; the needs and possibilities of the shipyards were neglected and the yards fell into obsolescence.

Nova Scotia, although it is backward, unproductive and poor today in comparison with Norway, was much richer than Norway at the turn of the century. Soon after coal and iron exports boomed, agricultural exports boomed too, particularly apples, sheep and cattle. Halifax, the chief city, boomed with the boom in exports and prospered as a coaling station for the British Navy, a base for the Canadian armed forces, a university town and a service center for its hinterland. Otherwise it developed little. It then stagnated, and its economy today is meager indeed, especially considering that it is the metropolis of all Atlantic Canada. Its most successful enterprise has been the Bank of Nova Scotia. It is one of the country's five great nationwide banks, and as such has been one of the major forces in shaping not only Nova Scotia's economy but also that of the country as a whole. In 1837, only five years after the bank was started, it had begun expanding into what is now central Canada.

Perhaps, had Norway hit on deposits of coal and iron when Nova Scotia did, it would have neglected industry too. But the fact is that it kept its one important industry of the time, shipbuilding, up to date—indeed, more than up to date in the sense that shipbuilding provided a market for a stream of Norwegian improvements and innovations in manufacturing. Poor as Norway was, and small though its population was, its domestic market *in the form of its shipping industry,* was solvent enough and large enough to support manufacturing in its service.

There is an important principle here that transcends the particularity of shipbuilding. It is this: Norway then, as it does now, managed to put its export work to double economic use. On the one hand, Norway's exports earn imports, just as Canada's exported resources do. But Norway's export work also affords a domestic market for tools of the trade. There is a big difference, on the one hand, between simply catching, canning and exporting fish, as Canada does, and on the other hand, catching, canning and exporting fish and also producing fish-canning machinery, as Norway does. Norway exports fish-canning machinery to us.

This basic strategy of development—this strategy of using its own producers of exports, as they emerge, as an existing, solvent, important domestic market for manufacturers and innovations—persists in Norway. For instance, Norway struck oil after Alberta did. But Norway has already invented and improved some tools of that trade which have become, in their turn, exports to other oil-producing countries. This has not been happening in Alberta. Norway has also become a leader in the creation of oil-field safety procedures and techniques, so that its experts in this area are in demand outside the country, too. One of Norway's other recent growth industries has been the manufacturing of nonpolluting electric furnaces for smelters. These were developed first for Norway's own producers. Now many hundreds have been supplied to other countries. The speed with which domestic producers' needs like these can be filled, as they become evident, is possible because by now so many chinks in the Norwegian economy have been filled. There are so many producers and suppliers of bits, pieces, tools, materials and services that innovators or other new producers require.

Here another principle of Norway's development comes into play. By concentrating as it did both on producing exports *and* on supplying them, Norway had a means of building up its general versatility at production. The versatility was a by-product. For instance, making forgings for one purpose develops skills and enterprises that can be drawn upon for other purposes. An economy that can produce improved fish-canning machinery can feasibly produce improved furniture-making machinery. Furthermore, when existing producers' work ramifies, so does the work of their suppliers, and by that means, too, the economy's versatility has increased. For instance, the shipbuilding branched into the development and manufacturing of ship-navigation devices, then ramified into airplane-navigation devices. In production of both, Norway became and remains a world leader. In turn, that work has provided a part of the domestic market for Norwegian microprocessing and computing equipment.

The economy's versatility at production, which was first built up significantly in Norway by making tools of the trades for exporters, is also the secret of Norway's ability to come up with many varieties of consumer goods economically for its small national population. Norway puts many of its manufactured imports, whether of producers' goods or consumer goods, to double economic use too. On the one hand, it consumes them, just as Canada does. But on the other hand, in due course it replaces many of them with its own production, as Canada does not. This is possible in Norway because the same economy which has become versatile at supplying producers is automatically versatile also at producing for Norway's own people. All those suppliers of bits, pieces, services and tools in the economy, all those skills and talents that have been developed, have made it possible to manufacture many consumer goods that were previously only imported or that previously people had to go without—and to make them efficiently. Furthermore, much of this indigenously designed and manufactured consumer goods becomes, as we have seen, export work in its own right. This is how it differs from Canada's branch-plant manufacturing which, as simply imitative, is inherently seldom exportable.

Norway's means of economic development is not peculiar to small countries. It is also the way large countries develop their economy. Large countries which fail to develop and make tools of the trades for their major producers, then for all manner of producers, do not develop economically, no matter how large their population is. Size of the country is beside the point where development is concerned. Rather, how the economy builds itself is of the essence; small countries like Norway have the same inherent opportunities as large ones.

Canadians have proved to be quite as economically able as Norwegians when it has happened that newly emerging producers in Canada have served as important domestic markets. For instance, the Canadian Broadcasting Corporation has consistently served as a market for much telecommunications equipment developed and manufactured in Canada. The consequence is that we have a splendid telecommunications industry. We export some of its products to Norway. But on the whole, this form of development has always been spotty and rare in Canada, and likely is destined to be so as long as the basic wealth of the country is thought to be what can be taken out of the ground and shipped away.

If the Canadian economic deficiencies summed up in the Ontario government's fact sheet really imply anything at all pertaining to the country's size, it is that the country is too big: in the sense that the same great economic and political institutions, with the same economically deadening assumptions, shape the entire country—no matter how urgently a given province or region may need to take a different approach, and no matter what kinds of fleeting opportunities for creating tools of the trades may actually be presenting themselves in this region or that.

But except in that sense, size is not the Canadian economic problem, nor would division of Canada into two smaller nations impose handicaps of size to development of manufacturing. Yet that argument is widely believed.

Early in 1980 the Toronto press carried a story about some hapless grocers in the Ontario town of Peterborough who had been compelled by the national government to convert their meat and produce scales to metric weight the year before and were now being permitted to revert to imperial weight. Describing the misfortunes and frustrations of one of these guinea-pig grocers, the report said: "Changing the meat scales [back to imperial] will probably cost about $3,000 and is being delayed because the old parts for it were thrown away by the scale company, and new ones must be sent from the United States."

The incident is revealing for two reasons. First, it presents a thumbnail description of everyday economic life in a country with a population twice the size of the Netherlands', three times the size of Sweden's, four times the size of Denmark's and more than five times the size of Norway's.

It also reminds us of how useless shortcuts or gimmicks can be, as a way of trying to overcome fundamental shortcomings. Some years ago the Canadian government put its faith into metric conversion as an important means of improving the country's feeble industrial export trade. Conversion was first undertaken in the mistaken belief that Americans would be doing likewise, but when this proved unfounded the program proceeded anyhow, on grounds that so much of the world market uses metric measurements. Starting with the daily newspaper weather reports, in due course specific dates for metric conversion were set for dozens upon dozens of items and practices: recipes in the newspaper food columns, road signs announcing distance and permitted speeds, architectural and engineering drawings, specifications for bricks and bolts, and bags of fertilizer, containers for cream, cat chow and cocktail mixes, problems in the algebra textbooks . . . By the time it was the meat's and produce bins' turn in the grocery stores, almost everyone realized that the connection with the country's industrial export trade was so far-fetched and in-

effectual that a pause was decreed. The point is that no gimmick, even when it is as expensive and sweeping as the change
in measurements has been, can substitute for an economy's
neglect to produce many of its own tools.

Canada's industrial predicament is real. But gimmicky
remedies and the gimmicky explanation that the market is
small are obfuscating. To hear the excuse of size turned into
an economic argument against Quebec separatism is disturb-
ing, not merely because it is a dishonest (or careless) argument, but because it is a disservice to all of Canada.

FIVE

Paradoxes of Size

Secessions are alarming to us if we think that making smaller things from bigger things is a step backward or downward. Is it? Does progression from bigger to smaller signify deterioration?

Clearly, sometimes it does. For instance, the Chrysler Corporation, if it survives as an automobile manufacturer, is going to be smaller than it used to be. Indeed, it is already smaller. To avoid bankruptcy it has had to sell off several subsidiaries it had bought up in the past. It has had to close down other plants, and it has had to lay off tens of thousands of workers, some in Canada. Chrysler's share of the automobile market has been shriveling; its deficits have been growing. Once the company was young, vital, growing, on the ball. It got bigger from year to year, appropriately—or so it seemed—while turning out bigger and bigger cars. Its recent history, however, is a glum tale of failures: failure to understand the limitations of what it had been doing, failure to pursue other possibilities successfully, failures in judgment and forecasting, failure to learn from its competitors.

Getting smaller often follows failure. As we all know, empires and nations, like automobile companies, can shrink or collapse because of decay. At the very moment when their power seems most invincible, their wealth most enviable, their achievements most astonishing, the worm is already at work, the decline is in the making, the center no longer holds, things begin insidiously to disintegrate. For an empire or a nation, just as for Chrysler, getting smaller or being cut up into pieces certainly can have connotations of dwindling, ebbing, sickening, decaying, disintegrating, failing.

But equally clearly, getting smaller or dividing does not always announce decay and forecast weakness. Let us return to industry for a minute, this time to the Standard Oil company instead of the Chrysler company. Back at the turn of the century, Standard Oil was not only a huge American corporation, but an outright monopoly. So ruthless were its methods of squeezing out or taking over competitors and so powerful had it become that in 1911, in a famous antitrust judgment, Standard Oil was dissolved into more than thirty different companies by order of the U.S. courts. Parts of the company were severed from one another. I am not going to name all the new corporations that came into being this way, but four of them are among the largest oil companies in the world: Standard Oil of New Jersey, which became Esso, now Exxon; Standard Oil of California; Standard Oil of New York, which became Socony, now Mobil; Standard Oil of Indiana, which became American or Amoco. Some of the others were Atlantic Refining Co., Anglo-American Oil Co. Ltd., Colonial Oil, Continental Oil, Standard Oil of Ohio, ten pipeline companies and a company building and operating railroad tank cars.

In short order some of the progeny became more profitable than the original company, and many of them individually came to exceed or rival it in size. The first three offspring I mentioned by name, Exxon, Standard Oil of California, and

Mobil, taken as a group, today dwarf the original Standard Oil.

I for one do not wish the oil companies well—or rather, I do not wish well their function of providing oil for fuel. I hope that particular function shrivels, dwindles and ebbs. But whatever happens to the oil industry in the future, that does not change this fact: when Standard Oil, a big entity, was reduced to smaller entities, the process at work was not the same as Chrysler's getting smaller.

Looking at an amoeba under the microscope, we may happen to catch it disintegrating, or we may see it being engulfed, eaten up whole, by another organism. But we may also see it dividing. Look, two amoebas where there was one. Making little ones out of big ones, then—whether amoebas, Standard Oil companies or even new nations like Norway—may mean not disintegration but birth, with the chance for new strength which birth implies.

In all economic life of any vigor, division in this sense happens constantly. Restaurant work is one of the largest employment categories in Canada, and has been one of the most rapidly growing in recent times. It is rife with amoebalike divisions. For one thing, restaurant chains keep splitting off new restaurants. Indeed, that is how they became chains in the first place—not by merely trying to add more tables, customers, cooks and cashiers into an ever bigger and bigger restaurant, but by multiplying into more restaurants. Besides that, restaurants give birth to independent progeny which are not branches or subsidiaries, but genuinely new enterprises. It is commonplace in Toronto, as elsewhere, for a chef from one restaurant to leave and start another of his own, quite independent of the first. People can learn a business one place, then cut the apron strings; the parents among the Toronto restaurants continue to thrive and so do most of the children.

In economic life the amoebas do not always divide into more amoebas. Sometimes the people who manage to split off new organizations from an old one do not duplicate the older company where they got their start; instead, they combine their experience with a new idea. An example would be a purchasing agent for a restaurant chain who becomes dissatisfied with the scales he buys, has a better idea for their design and teams up with a machinist from a tool-and-die company and a designer of microprocessor controls to start a new enterprise manufacturing food wholesalers' scales. The new enterprise would be not a reproduction of the parent enterprise, but a mutant.

Mutants are the most important form of division in economic life. The diversity of enterprises in Norway did not come out of thin air. They include many mutants. Existing enterprises are often open to new ideas, but most innovations take place in small, new companies. Indeed, that is why large, old companies so often buy up younger and smaller ones, for the power of size and the power to create are two different things.

In Canadian economic life, few mutations appear. Nor is there much simple reproduction of new, independent companies in manufacturing, the way there is in the restaurant business. If there were, Canadian manufacturing would be growing and vigorous; the spin-offs from older enterprises would imply not economic decay, but the contrary.

Sweden and Norway separated at a time when they were both vital—as their subsequent histories proved. That is why it is misleading to think of a separation such as theirs as a case of disintegration. "Big things turning into smaller things" has two different and opposite meanings. One implies decay and disintegration, the other implies birth and renewal of vigor. Once we understand this, we can make more theoretical sense out of Norway's separation from Sweden and the vitality released in both countries after the separation.

I have tried to keep away from speculative thinking for the most part, sticking instead to how things are in real life. But the thought that new nations are sometimes products of disintegration, of weakened, worn-out empires, but sometimes the opposite—products of a healthy birth—raises a speculative question about today's large nations. When we look at what has happened to sovereignties of the past, whether they were empires with scattered possessions or very large nations, we see that one and all they invariably reached a point when they behaved like decaying and disintegrating organisms, from ancient Persia to modern Britain. But must this always happen? Must the people of large sovereignties always be doomed to helplessness in the face of intractable problems, and to the eventual certainty of irreversible decline with all its hardships, waste and loss? Or is the division of great nations, undertaken before decay has proceeded too far to be irreversible, a means by which vitality could be renewed? As it is, of course, great nations are extremely resistant to divisions or secessions until and unless disintegration takes the choice out of their hands —and by then all their parts are apt to be devitalized.

Bigness means power, but only as long as the bigness is combined with vitality—no longer. Power is the attribute of bigness that makes bigness attractive to people. Admiration of bigness because of its power tends to make us overlook its inherent weakness: practicality is not the long suit of bigness. For one thing, big organizations, whether nations or enterprises, can make mistakes, just as small ones can, and when they do, the mistakes will be big ones, with big consequences. The Chrysler company, it is said, is too big to let fail. The consequences are too big for the company or even the country to admit failure, even if in fact it has failed.

Small organizations also make mistakes and fail, but in the sum of things these can more easily be absorbed, written off, taken in stride. Perhaps this has something to do with Europe's long hold upon vitality, which has confounded so many predictions of its imminent decay: all of those relatively small countries, all of them making their mistakes—frequently terrible mistakes—but not all making the same mistakes at the same time with the same consequences.

An English nursery rhyme says this:

> If all the seas were one sea,
> What a great sea that would be!
> If all the trees were one tree,
> What a great tree that would be!
> And if all the axes were one axe,
> What a great axe that would be!
> And if all the men were one man,
> What a great man that would be!
> And if the great man took the great axe,
> And cut down the great tree,
> And let it fall into the great sea,
> What a splish-splash that would be!

About half a century ago the English biologist J.B.S. Haldane wrote a delightful short essay called "On Being the Right Size." He pointed out, among other things, that sheer size has much to do with the equipment an animal must have. For instance, an insect, being so small, does not need an oxygen-carrying bloodstream. The oxygen its cells require can be absorbed by diffusion. Being larger means an animal must take on an oxygen-distributing and -pumping system to reach all the cells.

A relatively large animal, he also explained, has a relatively large mass in proportion to its surface area. The larger the animal, the greater the disproportion between the mass where the heat from oxidation is generated, and the surface area through which heat can escape. Big animals are thus inherently better equipped to withstand arctic and subarctic cold; they can more easily keep warm than small animals. But it also follows that large animals need special devices to dispose of internally generated heat before it becomes fatal: like sweat glands for cooling by evaporation, or the bizarre ears which increase the elephant's surface, or cooling, area.

Haldane presents us with an interesting principle about animal size: big animals are not big because they are complicated; rather, they have to be complicated because they are big. This principle, it seems to me, also applies to institutions, governments, companies, organizations of all sorts. The larger they are, the more complicated they must be. They are big because they produce a huge output of telephones, say, or have a lot of welfare clients, or govern a big population. Whatever the reason for expansion, the large size creates complications. Big organizations need coordinators, liaison people, prescribed channels of communication, administrators, supervisors of supervisors, whole extra departments devoted to serving the organization itself. A small organization can get along without a bureaucracy. A big one cannot.

Bigness and the complications that go along with it have their price, but can be worth it. The human brain—with its unfathomable numbers of cells for storing, sorting, cross-referencing and retrieving words, and doing so many other things too—is so complicated that it remains incomprehensible to us. Our brains' intricate capacities exact many prices which animals with smaller brains escape. We must use exorbitant amounts of fuel to maintain our brains and the services for them; we seem to be subjected to more mental illnesses than chickens or cows; we have to be born in an exceedingly helpless state in order to emerge before the head is too big for the birth canal; we have very extended childhoods compared with other animals, which can be hard on parents, and so on.

Just so, many jobs in this world can only be done or can best be done by large units. It is as simplistic to jump to the conclusion that something smaller is necessarily better than something bigger as it is to suppose the reverse. The point is that there is always a price to be paid for bigness. It would be too bad, or so I think, if we had only little villages or towns. But big cities exact a price, many prices; the extended and complicated physical, economic and social conditions their very size brings about have to be kept constantly in good working order, on pain of breakdown.

People who do not understand what I am calling Haldane's principle are forever being disappointed that making big units out of many smaller units seldom saves money. They think consolidation gives economies of scale. Sometimes, of course, this works, if the consolidated units really are small to begin with, and the aggregation of them not very large. But otherwise, the costs of added complications exact a price. When the government of Metropolitan Toronto was formed, combining some of the previously duplicated functions of government in what is now the city and five boroughs, the cost of government did not decline because of economies of scale. Costs rose. Even though unnecessary duplications of function were eliminated, other new functions and jobs had to be added just to make the larger bureaucracies of the larger police, school, traffic and social-service systems work. If all the functions of government in the city and five boroughs were to be amalgamated into a single all-purpose Metro government, we may be sure costs would soar.

In the United States a new President, when he takes office, usually sets forth as one of his aims simplification of the federal bureaucracy. Much highly skilled effort has gone into those attempts at reorganization and cost cutting. But the notable results have been that the attempts themselves have imposed additional costs and new complications. New bureaucracies have to be set up, or old ones expanded, to study the problems of reorganization, work out proposals and try to carry them out. Shift the old arrangements though they may, the reorganizations reduce neither costs nor complications of the federal bureaucracies. The size of the country and the centralization of its government require very big bureaucracies, which in turn require tremendous complications; the repeated reorganization schemes are, themselves, only further manifestations of those complications, not a cure for them. The high costs, the inflexibility of the bureaucracies, and their complexity are prices of scale.

One of the most exasperating and destructive costs of bigness is that sometimes the complications become so excessive that they are stifling: they interfere with the very purposes an organization is intended to serve. A hospital architect has told me that a hospital in Canada can be designed, built and put into operation in roughly two years' less time than a comparable hospital in the United States. The added costs of those two extra years' time and effort are of course large. Furthermore, the hospitals are apt not to be quite comparable in some sense because the same red tape that takes two extra years to untangle in the United States also precludes many sensible decisions, second thoughts and solutions to problems that can sometimes be undertaken in Canada. The differences in red tape, he says, are in large part owing to the fact that in the United States the huge federal government gets into the act with all its own complicated requirements—financing formulas and reviews, for example, all its own necessarily ponderous and complicated ways of doing things—and these are added to whatever complications are injected by the state, the municipality and the hospital administration itself. In Canada, the provincial governments, not Ottawa, take responsibility.

An Ontario civil servant told me a few years ago a similar tale about complications, this one concerning the clean-up of Lake Ontario. On our side of the border the work proceeded according to a timetable set up by international agreement. On the American side the similar work of building sewage-treatment plants fell far behind the timetable. The problem, he said, was not lack of money for the American part of the work, nor lack of will or interest either. People there had been working, in their own way, quite as hard as the Canadians. They were struggling with red tape. Red tape is the way we commonly describe complications of size that have become stifling.

Many jobs for which we have come to think that very large outfits are necessary—just because that is the way they are being handled—can be done as well by smaller organizations, indeed can sometimes be done better. When the Canadian postal system was smaller, had less mail to handle, it delivered the mail more swiftly and reliably. I think our postal system has become like the human brain in the sense that the post office itself is no longer able to understand its own complications. One of the things I look forward to if Quebec ever does separate is two smaller postal systems instead of what we now have. (Small countries have their own postal system; we do not see that as being extravagant or representing unnecessary duplication.) In the meantime, of course, much important Canadian mail is now no longer entrusted to the postal system. It turns out that small, hence less complicated, courier services are more reliable and swift, and even though they were supposed to be illegal and for a time were hounded and prosecuted, they flourished because they had become a sheer necessity. Some in Toronto now charge only 15 cents a letter in comparison with the official 17 cents, but it is their reliability and speed that make them so valuable. On occasion, to the government's embarrassment, government departments have been caught using them.

Many Americans take it for granted that telephone service has to be consolidated in a huge organization to be efficient. When I tell American acquaintances that the province of Alberta has long owned a separate telephone system, and that I can vouch from experience for its first-rate efficiency, they are amazed. They become downright incredulous when they hear that within Alberta the city of Edmonton owns yet a different and separate telephone system and that it works with first-class efficiency too. I hardly dare tell them that the two systems have an excellent reputation for creating improvements in service and equipment—but they do.

In New York, people have been pointing out for a couple of generations that the amount of money spent per pupil in the public schools is larger than the amount per pupil spent in many fine private schools with smaller classes. At first thought it is hard to imagine, short of assuming embezzlement, how the discrepancies between what is paid for and what is delivered can be explained. But if one explores the New York public school system's administration and sees the burden of overhead the vast consolidated system supports, the costs become understandable. These are costs of size, not corruption. Perhaps we can speak of the corruption of size. Decentralization of the school system was undertaken about a decade ago in New York. But in practice, decentralization meant new layers of administration and complication within the central organization, because the central organization was retained too. As Marshall McLuhan has said, you can't decentralize centrally.

Where national governments are concerned, a traditional way of keeping size and its complications under control has been federalism. Most large nations have employed federal systems in one form or another, and so have some very small ones, such as Switzerland. Of course there have been other reasons for federalism too. It provides varying degrees of autonomy for autonomy's own sake, but one use of it has been to try to keep big government and centralized government in hand.

Federalism has been falling on bad days in many places. The Soviet Union has federalism in form, but in fact is exceedingly centralized in its management and decisions. The United States has federalism in form, but in fact has converted itself into a unitary state where all but the most minor and inherently local matters—and even some of those—must be traipsed through centralized corridors of power.

Centralization of national governments has been gathering force in most of this century and has been intensifying swiftly in our own time. When centralization is combined with increased responsibilities taken on by government, as has also been happening, the result is very big government.

Not all countries have embraced this combination. Switzerland and Japan are outstanding exceptions. Both have relatively few national programs. Canada has also resisted extreme centralization because Quebec, Ontario, Alberta and British Columbia have insisted on considerable provincial autonomy. Thus Canada retains a federal system in fact as well as in form. Nevertheless, elephantiasis threatens us, too. Ottawa's employees have increased by more than 50 percent just since 1968.

Almost everywhere in the world, bureaucratic complications have now become so intractable as to defy either solution or understanding. Many intelligent, industrious and well-intentioned people in government are spending their lives creating messes, futilities and waste because they cannot avoid doing so. The complications are labyrinthine. The red tape is stifling. The vast, unwieldy organizational bulks are inflexible, impossible to put on the right track when they have nosed onto the wrong. Arrangements like this do not seem to offer a promising future.

If we take Haldane's principle seriously, as I think we must, increased centralization of government ought not to be combined with added or multiplied governmental responsibilities. On the contrary, added governmental responsibilities ought logically to be combined with looser federalism, or else with secessions. Certainly it seems that the only promising arrangement for busy governments, if that is what we need or want, is small nations.

To go back to the size of animals once more, some become so bulky that no conceivable complications can contend with the hazards of their size. They must have very special environments to survive. In the heat of the day, the hippopotamus immerses itself in water, only its nostrils emerging. The great whales could never have attained their huge size except in water; otherwise their own heat would have killed them. There is an analogy to be found here, appropriately a chilling one. The biggest and most thoroughly centralized governments have always, finally, required the special environment of oppression to continue to maintain themselves. And some could never have attained their great size at all had they not grown in that environment.

SIX
Duality and Federation

Canada's constitution is a law that was passed in 1867 by the British Parliament, and to this day it is called the British North America Act. In reality, the act was not British. It was prepared by a group of Canadians now known as the Fathers of Confederation, led by John A. Macdonald (later Canada's first prime minister), who worked out the form of government they wanted for a unified Canada and got what they asked. Curiously, they omitted to include a procedure for amendment, evidently assuming that changes, if necessary, could be adopted in Britain in the same routine fashion as the basic act. Thus, formal Canadian constitutional changes are legitimized by another government in another country.

The persistence of that quaint and antiquated arrangement is not owing to infatuation with tradition, but rather to an impasse within Canada. "Patriating the constitution" has long been an aim of Canada's government and political parties. Reports and studies by the dozens have proposed patriation and revisions, and there has been no dearth of constitutional conventions either, most recently the Victoria Conference of 1971, called by Prime Minister Pierre Trudeau. But all to no avail. Agreement has not been reached on an indigenous means of amending the existing constitution, much less on writing a new one. To open up the subject of the constitution at all is to open up such a can of worms that each time it has been tried the lid has soon been clapped back on. Another attempt is starting in 1980.

Quebec's role in the country has been the chief difficulty. French Quebec's theory is that Canada is composed of two equal "founding peoples," English and French, and that Quebec embodies one of the two. This theory, which is embraced quite as tenaciously by nonseparatists in French Quebec as by separatists, demands that the constitution ought properly to recognize duality and to make it real and functional. For instance, to put both founding peoples on equal footing and to make the equality functional would mean that Quebec must have power unilaterally to veto proposed constitutional amendments even if they are wanted by the English majority. Quebecois believe they need that power to protect Quebec's cultural, judicial and legislative interests.

But Canada is composed of ten provinces, not two. The understanding of the other provinces is that they have a federation and within it are on an equal footing under the law. While the other provinces agree that Quebec should be treated as a special case in some respects, they draw the line at Quebec's legally having unique and disproportionate powers over *them*. The Victoria Conference of 1971 tried ingeniously to get around the amendment-veto problem by singling out a second province, Ontario, to be given veto power too. Duality was thus to be expressed by equality of English Ontario and French Quebec. The compromise might have been agreed upon had not Quebec been dissatisfied with many other proposals. But even as a necessary compromise such an arrangement does not sit well with the other provinces because of course it proposes dividing the country into another type of duality: first-class and second-class provinces, those with peculiar powers over the others and those without. It negates the meaning of Confederation, both in theory and fact.

The most recent proposal for amendment procedure, this one put forward by Quebec federalists under the leadership of Claude Ryan in January 1980, separates constitutional clauses into two varieties: those that could be amended by the provinces acting as an ordinary federation, and those—all the really important ones—that would be "shielded" or "entrenched." Amendments to the latter would need consent of "provinces which constitute or have constituted in the past at least 25% of the Canadian population." Since only Quebec and Ontario meet that criterion, and since none of the others remotely approaches it now, here is duality again at the expense of federation, the only concession being that at some time in the future this or that additional province might conceivably enter the ranks of the first-class.

One can understand why the Canadian constitution is still, as this is written, being amended in Britain.

In practice, most changes actually occur informally; they are formalized or not after they have been established by usage. For instance, annual federal-provincial conferences have become almost as vital to the actual workings of the government as annual sessions of Parliament. Presumably they would get some recognition in a patriated constitution; theoretically, the existing constitution could recognize and legitimize them by amendment. Neither has been possible because either attempt would promptly open up the insoluble issue of Quebec's special powers within formalized conferences.

The difficulties posed by amendment procedures are as nothing compared to the difficulties that duality poses for other procedures and other constitutional arrangments. We can get a sense of these by glancing at a few of the other features included among the recent Ryan proposals.

To create judicial duality, the proposal is that the Chief Justice of the nine-member Supreme Court be alternately selected from Quebec and from all-the-other-provinces-lumped-together. For consideration of ordinary cases, only three of the other eight judges would need to be from Quebec, but in cases involving constitutional issues, four of the eight would have to be from Quebec if that is requested by the national government, any provincial government or any individual.

How to express duality in cultural matters? The Ryan scheme proposes a permanent committee of delegates from the provinces, composed equally of English and French representatives with Quebec guaranteed 80 percent of the French delegates. Any acts of Parliament bearing on language, the National Gallery of Art, broadcasting, the archives, grants to the arts, and so on, would constitutionally have to be ratified by the committee, and so would all senior appointments to Crown (public and quasi-public) corporations touching on cultural matters. It is easy to understand why even federalists in Quebec believe their province must possess these disproportionate powers—relative to the other provinces—but the fact remains that they would be disproportionate and that they would affect many matters of vital interests to Canadians outside Quebec.

One can understand why patriating the constitution has become so difficult.

But difficulties in getting agreement on a new document are as nothing compared to the probable difficulties that would arise in trying to make a hybrid dual-federal system work. Another of the changes proposed by the Ryan group is for a new organ of government, a Federal Council. Its voting members would be composed of delegations from the provinces, serving at the pleasure of their provincial government, and they would be required by law to vote as provincial blocs, according to the instructions sent them from their provincial government.

This council would possess enormous powers over Parliament. For example, it would have to ratify "all central government proposals affecting the fundamental equilibrium of the federation," all appropriations by Parliament, all senior judicial and executive appointments, all treaties affecting provincial affairs, many matters concerned with regional development; and it would also advise Parliament in advance on its wishes in these matters and on other matters not requiring council ratification.

Quebec would be constitutionally guaranteed a quarter of the voting membership, regardless of demographic changes (Quebec is currently losing population, and western Canada is growing more rapidly than other parts of the country), and the smaller provinces would be guaranteed overrepresentation to compensate for their smallness. All the others, meaning Ontario and most of western Canada, would be underrepresented.

A two-thirds majority of votes would be required for ratifications. In practice that would mean, of course, that a third of the body could paralyze everything. When one couples that power of the minority with the underrepresentations of the west and Ontario, one may imagine the forced deals, the frustrations, the angers, threats and cries of foul that the scheme would inevitably breed. But it is merely an attempt to insert the principle of duality—or something which as a practical matter would approach it—into the legislative processes of the national government.

The proposed council has been described variously by

proponents in Quebec as an evolution of the federal-provincial conferences, an evolution of Canada's powerless and honorific Senate, and a new creation modeled on the German Bundestag. Whatever its pedigree, it has also been described by Ryan as "the pylon"—the indispensable, central, structural member—of "renewed federalism" acceptable to Quebec.

Indeed, from the viewpoint of Quebec the proposed council is, if anything, generous in the compromise it makes with full and complete duality. But looked at from the viewpoint of the underrepresented provinces, it would be unfair on the face of it and rigged, to boot, to entrench government by minority rule. From the viewpoint of Parliament and national agencies the proposal is, in a word, appalling.

Under normal circumstances, little or no attention would likely have been paid to proposals such as these outside of Quebec. But they have become significant for two reasons. First, they represent the most ingenious, the most responsible, detailed and rounded attempt yet made to formulate a Canadian government based on the theory of duality. And second, English Canada found itself in the position of relying upon these proposals and their chief proponent, Ryan, as a means of defeating separatist sentiment in Quebec's referendum on sovereignty-association, held in May 1980.

The basic reason that English Canada must heed Quebec's theory of duality and the rearrangements it implies is that the possibility always lurks that Quebec might decide to secede if it cannot be placated.

The leader of separatist sentiment, René Lévesque, has been premier of Quebec since 1976 when the Parti Québecois, which he helped found in 1967, won the provincial elections, defeating the provincial Liberal Party. Lévesque, the son of a country lawyer from a small, predominantly English town on the Gaspé Peninsula, has been a well-known and much admired figure in the province for some twenty-five years, first as a radio and television commentator on national and world affairs, and subsequently as provincial minister of natural resources in Liberal Party governments of the early 1960s. He left that party after his belief crystallized that Quebec should seek independence, and when he had become convinced that to convert the party to his view was hopeless.

Because he is small-boned and short, Lévesque is often described as wispy, but there is nothing ethereal about his drive, nor does his intent and deeply furrowed face suggest wispiness. He is a tireless explainer, more in the manner of a teacher than a showman or orator, and he has the inspired teacher's gift for holding his pupils spellbound as he analyzes and explains. His government has been untouched by scandal, and one widely held view, both in English Canada and Quebec, is that his party was voted into power less as a vehicle for separatist sentiment than as a means of getting an honest and competent provincial government.

Lévesque and his running mates carefully refrained from making separatism an issue in the 1976 election. Nevertheless, one of Lévesque's pledges had been that before his government ran for election again, the question of whether the people of Quebec wanted their government to try negotiating sovereignty-association would be put to a vote so they could decide the question themselves, by referendum.

The pledge threw alarm into English-speaking Canada; the response of the national government, the government of Ontario and of most of the other provinces was, "We will negotiate no such thing!" But still, what if Quebec voters should answer *Oui* in the referendum? The rest of Canada recognized that as a practical matter the results of a Quebec referendum could not really be ignored.

The prospect of a possible *Oui* vote was even more alarming, if anything, to opponents of separatism within Quebec. To meet the danger, one of the province's most esteemed citizens took over leadership of the provincial Liberal Party and devoted himself to rebuilding it as an effective voice for Quebec federalists.

Claude Ryan, who is French despite his name, has been well known and highly respected in Quebec for some twenty years, first as editor, then publisher, of *Le Devoir,* a leading Montreal newspaper. His reputation for integrity, like Lévesque's, is impeccable. He is a man of great dignity, with large, lustrous and expressive eyes, and in Quebec he is thought of as the very embodiment of a proper paterfamilias. He is the sort of person to whom parties in a dispute turn, trusting his fairness and judgment, and his influence in the affairs of Quebec has been a product of these good offices and of his editorials in defense of Quebecois interests, particularly in cultural matters. He is also, it turns out, a very talented politician. His work of rebuilding and rejuvenating the Liberal Party, down at its grass roots, has been so successful that the party has won all seven provincial parliamentary by-elections held in the past year or so, some of them in ridings which the Parti Québecois carried overwhelmingly in 1976; he is expected by many political experts to be the province's next premier.

Although Ryan is a Quebec nationalist in the sense of being an unwavering defender of Quebec's right and need to defend and develop its own culture, and to be autonomous in shaping its own social policies and programs, he is anything but a separatist. He believes that for Quebec to separate from Canada would be a wild and ruinous course. In particular, he is convinced that Quebec needs the Canadian banking system, the country's nationwide, highly mobile capital, and access to the national government's subsidies.

With Claude Ryan in charge of the antiseparatist political

forces, English Canada breathed a sigh of relief—all the more so after Ryan let it be known in 1979 that he had set up a constitutional committee in the provincial Liberal Party and that it was laboring to prepare a realistic alternative to sovereignty-association. It would be published, he indicated, before the dread Parti Québecois referendum, and as an alternative it would give Quebec voters good reason to vote *Non*. English Canada began banking rather heavily on the Ryan proposals, sight unseen; much comment in the press alluded kindly to the document even before it was forthcoming.

In the latter part of 1979, as Ryan began showing the proposals to premiers in other parts of Canada to try to line up their support, little winds of disquiet began to blow across the land; nothing much, just hints of doubts. In the meantime, the Quebec government issued its White Paper on Sovereignty-Association and announced that the referendum was only months away. English Canada could not afford doubts about the Ryan proposals; anticipation of them built up, and at length, in January 1980, they were published with great fanfare. They are popularly called the beige paper.

Muted consternation! Consternation because of what they were. Muted because for English Canada to say forcefully that it found them unacceptable might undercut the *Non* vote in the referendum. Ryan was reported in the press to be "rattled by the polite, but generally noncommittal response" he had received from the politicians of English Canada. His position was that they must understand that the Quebecois are not pleased with the status quo, and that if his proposals for duality or something much like them are not accepted, he cannot answer for the disillusioned reaction in Quebec.

One bemused spectator, J. D. Morton, a professor of law at the University of Toronto, likened the situation to the routine of a Mutt and Jeff detective team working over a suspect.

... Mutt becomes more and more hostile and threatening. Jeff intervenes to restrain him and suggests that Mutt leave for a while until he cools down. Mutt leaves and Jeff acts protectively toward the subject, offering him cigarets, coffee and understanding. At the same time, the subject is reminded that Mutt is not far away and that the degree of control exercised by Jeff over Mutt is tenuous in the extreme.

Not infrequently the technique is successful. The subject turns to and pours out his heart to his protector . . .

It would be ridiculous to suggest that Lévesque and Ryan are consciously applying the Mutt and Jeff technique to the rest of Canada. Nevertheless, what occurs in art may well occur in nature. As in the case of the detectives, the goals of the two actors seem remarkably similar . . .

For working over Quebec, Canada and Ryan also made up a Mutt and Jeff team. There, Canada served as the implacable member, Ryan the sympathetic one again, but both wanted the same thing: to extract a *Non* vote from Quebec on the referendum. Ryan's catchword for his proposals was "renewed federalism." The federal government and English Canada took up the phrase. A vote against sovereignty-association was presented as a vote for "renewed federalism."

The wording of the referendum question read:

The Government of Quebec has made public its proposal to negotiate a new agreement with the rest of Canada, based on the equality of nations;

This agreement would enable Quebec to acquire the exclusive power to make its laws, levy its taxes and establish relations abroad—in other words, sovereignty—and at the same time to maintain with Canada an economic association including a common currency;

No change in political status resulting from these negotiations will be effected without approval by the people through another referendum;

On these terms, do you give the Government of Quebec the mandate to negotiate the proposed agreement between Quebec and Canada?

Apart from one meeting that degenerated into brief fisticuffs, the thirty-five-day campaign was fought solely by argument. That a country would countenance a vote on separatism was remarkable in itself; that the process could take place without violence was even more so. Both facts spoke to the distinctive national temperament of Canada, and particularly to how profoundly it differs from the United States.

Prime Minister Pierre Trudeau said that he and his government would not negotiate sovereignty-association, but promised that a *Non* victory would bring a new constitution. The premiers of the other provinces agreed: with one voice they declared that *Oui* could result only in deadlock and stalemate, while *Non* would swiftly bring "renewed federalism" and big changes. The election itself conveyed that urgency because voters under the age of forty overwhelmingly favored *Oui*. Old and young taken together, the French vote was almost evenly divided. The *Non* side's large margin of victory (59.5 percent of the vote) was granted by the fifth of the population which is non-French and which voted *Non* almost solidly.

During the campaign, nobody discussed the concrete meaning of the promised "renewed federalism," with good reason. To Trudeau, who has always been a strong centralist, it means major powers must rest in a strong federal parliament. To the poor Maritime Provinces, it also means strong central government with reinforced commitments to spreading the national wealth. To Ontario, it means as little substantive change as possible. To the west, and perhaps to Newfoundland, it means increased provincial powers and a weaker central government. To Quebec, it means recognition of duality. All this must be compromised and resolved—or not—in a constitutional struggle which will likely occupy the next several years.

The referendum result still leaves English Canada and Quebec in the predicament of being able to live harmoniously neither with each other nor without each other. The issue of how to combine duality of French and English Canada with federation of ten provinces remains insoluble because it is inherently insoluble. To adopt the theory that the country consists of two peoples highly unequal in numbers, and yet equal, or almost so, in their powers over the country as a whole, is to make federation unworkable. But to retain workable federation means that Quebec's claim to equality with English-speaking Canada in the organs and organizations of government cannot be satisfied.

Lévesque and his colleagues are the only political leaders in the country who have admitted that this constitutional problem is insoluble, have faced the implications of that fact, and have tried to come to grips with a different solution—another way in which Quebec and English Canada can live without each other and yet with each other.

SEVEN

Sovereignty-Association: Connectors

The phrase sovereignty-association has two elements meaning "independent" and "connected," and thus it is a thumbnail description of the human condition itself. As we all know, it is not easy for us as individuals to juggle those elements, juggle our individual nature and our social nature without doing unacceptable damage to either. Customs, traditions and philosophies of innumerable sorts help us in this juggling act. Even so, we have to practice and work at it as long as we live, forever making subtle readjustments and corrections to try to keep some balance between our independence and our connectedness.

In nature, the wolf and the deer have become a famous metaphor of separateness and connectedness. Since independence implies conscience, conscious will and consideration of the future, we can hardly call the wolf and deer "independent" and connected, but they engage in the separate and connected juggling acts of nature, balancing the well-being of each species with the interdependent systems on which survival also depends. Constant readjustments are necessary, as when the size of the herd must readjust to winter food supplies; subtle corrections occur as when the wolves contract, expand or shift their territories with shifts in the populations of deer.

Governments and nations, like the rest of us, have their juggling acts too—their ways of being both independent and connected. A synonym for René Lévesque's phrase "sovereignty-association" might be Allied Powers, except for its historical connotations. Or we could try United States, United Nations or United Kingdom. All appropriated already; it is the same with League of Nations. We might try Group of Independents, except that it sounds like a society of separate and connected artists or perhaps an organization of retail grocery stores. Or we might try Canadian League, except that it sounds like a hockey association. Or perhaps simply Confederation, except that this is already used to mean Canada's separate and connected provinces inside a sovereign state. We seem to be running out of ways of saying "independent and connected governments." But of course we can always invent new names for new tries, as Lévesque has done.

Governments, like individuals, have the help of customs and traditions in their juggling acts. Nations have representative national assemblies, constitutions, divisions of powers, courts to adjudicate national rights, states rights, municipal rights, and so on. These are primarily for their domestic juggling acts.

Internationally, nations use embassies, diplomatic protocol, treaties, trade missions, cultural exchanges, armed forces, spy organizations and double agents, world courts, world banks, summit meetings, international assemblies, passports, maritime law, letters of credit—all as devices to juggle independence with connectedness to other nations.

Nations have a double juggling act, then: domestic and international. The first city-state that ever conquered or engulfed another and made it a province or dependency, back before history was being written, was from that moment engaged in a double juggling act, and this is what has faced most governments since. That double task, domestic and international, is difficult to an extreme.

When nations draw connections too tight domestically, the consequences are internal oppression, or else the highly complicated bureaucracies of highly centralized governments, or both. Yet if connections break down domestically, the consequence is civil disorder. In extreme cases, the consequences are collections of rival war-lord regimes, such as those that flickered in China between the collapse of the empire early this century and the reimposition of centralized rule by the Communist government, or the war-lord regimes we call feudalism which took over when the center no longer held in the Western Roman Empire.

When nations draw the international connections too tightly, independence is compromised, as happened for example when Soviet troops entered Czechoslovakia in 1968 or when the United States and Britain masterminded a coup in Iran and installed their own creature, the Shah. But if connections break down internationally, trade in useful goods and in safe and protected movements of diplomats, merchants and other persons halt, and often enough there is war.

We must realistically suppose that nations will have to practice and work at their juggling acts interminably, both internationally and domestically. But to put it mildly, their acts can stand a lot of improvement, and therefore some necessarily cautious experimenting, such as is implied by the idea of sovereignty-association, hardly seems amiss.

Domestically, in federal systems, constitutions are the customary means of drawing up a balance between independence and connections. But in the case of a sovereignty-association, such as Lévesque proposes for Quebec, the appropriate means is negotiation between equally independent sovereignties, resulting in treaties. First, the basic framework of the connections must be negotiated and agreed upon. Then, in open-ended fashion, as occasion or need arises, further negotiations can lead to joint programs or projects like those that Norway and Sweden engage in, for example. Hence Lévesque's proposal that sovereignty-association be worked out through negotiation in the first place, then after that be fleshed out through further negotiation, is a sensible procedure.

The basic framework of a sovereignty-association must sort out the kinds of functions which, by treaty, are to be shared or maintained mutually. I am going to look at Lévesque's proposals and reasoning from the point of view of workability of the basic framework he suggests. My chief source is his book, *My Quebec*. The ideas set forth there were, with little change, incorporated in the Quebec government's 1979 White Paper on Sovereignty-Association.

Lévesque suggests five connectors. I will say, right off, that four of them seem to me to be right on the mark. But the fifth seems so ill-considered and unworkable that I am convinced it would automatically give rise to frictions and recriminations and would also undermine Quebec's independence. I think I see a possible way of overcoming the difficulty, which I will suggest. But first, let us look at the four connectors that ought to work.

The first one Lévesque proposes, and the basic one, is free trade between the associated sovereignties.

We are much preoccupied in Canada with the subject of foreign export trade, with the result that we have much more statistical data about our foreign exports and imports than about our own internal trade. That is true of most other countries too. But Statistics Canada has also made two surveys of internal trade. These were analyses of the destinations of Canadian manufactured goods. One survey was made in the late 1960s, the other in 1974. Here is what they tell us:

By far the greatest markets for Canadian manufactured goods are within Canada itself. In 1974, more than half the goods found their outlets in the provinces where they were made. In addition to that, more than a quarter found their markets in other provinces. Only 21 percent of Canada's manufactured goods were exported, chiefly to the United States, and chiefly from Ontario. Ontario alone accounts for 82 percent of all Canadian manufactures sold to the United States and for roughly comparable proportions of Canadian-made goods exported to other countries too. (While some of the other provinces engage in a large foreign trade, it is overwhelmingly in resources, as much of Ontario's foreign trade is also.) But even for Ontario's manufactures, Canadian markets are vital. They absorb two-thirds; much of that market, of course, is within Ontario itself.

The trade between provinces follows the pattern one might expect from looking at a map: neighboring provinces tend to be one another's best customers. Beginning in the west, British Columbia and Alberta are each other's chief interprovincial customers. The central west is split down the middle. Saskatchewan's best customer for its meager production of manufactured goods, apart from itself of course, is Alberta. Manitoba's best customer is Ontario. Ontario and Quebec are each other's best customers. Nova Scotia is the best customer of Prince Edward Island, Ontario the best customer of New Brunswick, and Quebec the best customer of Newfoundland and Nova Scotia.

The biggest interprovincial trade in manufactured goods is that between Quebec and Ontario. It has increased a good deal in recent times, as the city markets of Montreal, on the one hand, and Toronto and the Golden Horseshoe, on the other, have both grown. The trade doubled in value just between 1967 and 1974. During that time, Ontario's exports of goods to Quebec rose by 88 percent, while Quebec's to the faster-growing markets of Ontario rose by 122 percent in value. Of course, those increases are in considerable part owing to inflation; if there were figures for growth in volume, they would be much lower. Nevertheless, the increases in value of manufactured goods traded between Ontario and Quebec go far beyond gains in value of manufactured goods exported to foreign countries. Quebec is no province's poorest customer for Canadian-made goods, not even British Columbia's.

The trade links between Quebec and the rest of Canada—especially with Ontario and the Atlantic Provinces—would still exist if Quebec were to become independent. They would *have* to exist. Canada's manufacturing economy, already so slender, would collapse in their absence, or something close to it. There is no point in fantasizing how Canada could cut off trade with an independent Quebec, treat it the way the United States treated Cuba after the Cuban revolution. The consequence would be intolerable economic privation for all concerned.

Of course, some people talk as if an independent Quebec could be punished for its independence—blockaded, ignored or isolated. From time to time the press reports sentiments like this: a proposed new corridor road across Maine would speed truck and tourist traffic between the Atlantic Provinces and central Canada and it would take on added importance—here is the kicker—in the event of separation of Quebec from Confederation.

The man who said that is a past president of the Atlantic Provinces Chamber of Commerce. Of course, much traffic between Quebec and the Maritimes already runs through Maine because the route is shorter and more convenient in spite of the nuisance of crossing international boundaries. There spoke a man who accepts such border crossings with equanimity, even with some enthusiasm—yet is dismayed that people and goods could traverse an independent Quebec. Such remarks are emotional, not rational, comments on trade and trade routes. Yet even provincial premiers and cabinet ministers make spiteful and frivolous remarks in this vein. They must think it good politics, or perhaps their emotions really do get the better of their reason.

Owing to the geographical position of the Atlantic Provinces, with Quebec lying between them and central Canada, free and unimpeded flow of trade back and forth across Quebec, as well as into or out of Quebec, would be especially important to the Atlantic Provinces. Lévesque is quite right in identifying free trade as a practical link in a sovereignty-association framework. Because it would be mutually beneficial, and certainly workable, it would serve as a powerful connector.

The second connector he proposes is similar in principle: free travel of persons. He also proposes, as a possible point for negotiation, dual citizenship with joint issuance of Canadian-Quebec passports for foreign travel. Both of these connectors, free trade and free travel, would leave present trade and travel arrangements essentially as they are now. So would a customs union, or partial customs union, if that were included as Lévesque suggests.

The next two connectors entail some changes. These proposals are meant, as I read their meaning, to give assurances that the changes are not substantive or threatening.

The St. Lawrence River, over much of its course, runs solely through Quebec territory, yet of course it is vital to Ontario directly and to all the rest of Canada indirectly. So Lévesque has proposed a maritime community, which the White Paper spells out as a membership for Quebec, alongside Canada and the United States, on the International Joint Commission for the St. Lawrence Seaway.

His fourth connector is military and therefore deals with an inherently touchy subject—the more so because of Quebec's history of resisting conscription in World War I and conscription for overseas service in World War II. Lévesque proposes that Quebec participate in the same military alliances as Canada, which means participation in NATO and the joint Canadian-U.S. alliance called NORAD. Offhand, such a suggestion might seem logically to fall into a category of cooperative programs, but he includes it as part of the framework of association, as does the White Paper. I think he is correct to include it. A sovereignty such as Canada simply could not permit an associated sovereignty, such as Quebec, to take a different military line where defense arrangements are concerned. Nor could it possibly be in Quebec's interest to do so, either, if for no other reason than that Quebec's geographical position would make such a course impractical. Thus this is another essential of the basic framework.

Lévesque's last connector is his proposal that Canada and a sovereign Quebec share the same currency.

Such a proposal might have seemed plausible between 1945 and 1971, when what was called the Bretton Woods agreement on international currencies operated. That system, which was introduced on the initiative of the United States, was adopted by Canada and by much of Europe. It was an attempt to introduce fixed exchange rates between these currencies, which were all pegged to the U.S. dollar. Thus, they fluctuated little in relation to one another or, of course, in relation to the dollar itself. It was thought that this scheme would achieve international monetary stability. One of its advantages was that multinational corporations, like automobile manufacturers, for instance, could distribute various parts or engine-making plants and assembly plants through many different countries, based on advantageous labor costs or financing arrangements, without fearing that changes in international exchange rates would undercut their calculations. But under the cover of this artificially imposed stability, discrepancies among the real values of currencies were building up. None of the participating countries wanted the system to collapse. But in 1971 it did collapse because it had got so out of touch with what was really happening that it could no longer work.

For one thing, countries that were experiencing rapidly escalating rates of inflation at home were, in effect, exporting their inflation to other countries. As their money depreciated in value relative to other currencies, its exchange value should have dropped correspondingly. Since the exchange values were pegged, however, those adjustments could not be made, so the inflated currencies diluted the real value of uninflated currencies. When the U.S. currency became inflated owing to costs of the Vietnam war, among other things, all the countries to which the U.S. currency was pegged necessarily lost some value too. By buying foreign goods at prices which were actually too low and exporting at prices which were actually too high—considering the lowered real value of its currency —the United States was exporting some of the costs of the war and some of its domestic deficits to other economies.

The United States was not the only exporter of inflation under the Bretton Woods agreement, but the impact of its inflation was the most serious because the U.S. dollar was the anchor currency. Furthermore, the United States also began to run big deficits in its balance of trade. This discrepancy led to a vast oversupply of U.S. dollars in Europe, which made nonsense of European monetary reserves, since U.S. dollars were included among the bank reserves against which European loans were made.

From the mid-1960s, the system was heading for disaster; the collapse, when it finally came in 1971, created a financial crisis. It also initiated a period during which many currencies had to be abruptly and drastically revalued up or down.

Changes and adjustments between the various currencies to reflect national changes in trade, inflation and productivity relationships that had been taking place over a period of a quarter of a century had been dammed up. Nowadays, when it is convenient to blame all inflation on the oil-exporting countries, we sometimes forget that the depreciation of the U.S. dollar actually began in the 1960s and created havoc internationally.

Now, here is the important point we need to understand when considering the advisability of shared currencies: national policies of many kinds influence the value of a country's currency. Incomes within a country can easily be increased by social programs of many kinds, ranging from welfare payments and pensions to mandated rises in minimum wages, and by subsidy programs of many kinds to corporations, farmers, local governments. But if, at the same time, there is not a corresponding increase in production and productivity, then the money loses real value. We say too much money is chasing too few goods. Or we say the government is printing money for programs the economy cannot support.

National policies are also influential in determining a country's balance of trade with others, although the influence is often oblique. What an economy produces—and therefore may be capable of selling in foreign trade—is at least partially determined by national policies regarding investment of public money, regarding the kinds of development schemes favored and those that are discouraged, the activities government thinks it worthwhile to subsidize and those it thinks not worthwhile, the interest rates set by law or regulation, and by a country's tax policies, because all countries nowadays regard taxation not merely as a means of raising revenue but also as a means of favoring some economic activities and, if only by default, penalizing others. The almost diametrically different directions that the Canadian economy and the Norwegian economy have taken are in large part owing to the Canadian government's emphasis on exploitation and export of resources, and its policies for attracting branch plants, and the Norwegian government's assumption that wealth also consists of innovation, invention and development of indigenous manufacturing. These differing assumptions, and the differing policies that spring from them, have great influence upon the nature of Norway's foreign trade and of Canada's, and on each country's balance of trade.

That is not to say that these matters are uninfluenced by private investments and private successes and failures in production; both inflation and trade balances reflect nongovernmental acts too. But it is to say that government programs and policies are important indeed in most countries, including Canada, in creating inflation or deflation, influencing what is traded, influencing the size of trade imbalances; and in sum, the value of currencies. Because that is so, shared currencies are not really workable unless the governments that share a currency also share the government powers which can influence the value of the currency.

Lévesque wants Quebec to have full sovereignty over taxation, social policies and at least some military expenditures, over investment policies, borrowing policies and some policies concerned with use of private savings and accumulations of capital, over funds spent on public bureaucracies and subsidies, and many other matters that affect the value of a given currency relative to others. These are powers now largely, although not entirely, held by Ottawa. Indeed, Lévesque complains of exactly that when he says that Quebec does "not control the real economic levers which remain in the federal domain."

What Lévesque fails to confront is that the powers he wants for Quebec are powers that happen to influence the strength or weakness of a currency relative to others, and that also influence the value of a currency domestically. Suppose Canada and Quebec sometimes do become associated sovereignties, and suppose each really did then exercise independently the kinds of powers I have mentioned. Nowadays, when our currency falls on bad times, we blame Ottawa. Under double sovereignty with a shared currency, Ottawa and Quebec would be blaming each other. Unless everything went along marvelously, they would likely be furious with each other.

The answer to that—on which both Lévesque and the White Paper rely—is that the two governments could cooperate on managing the shared currency and act jointly on matters that affect it. Yes, so they could. But there goes independence.

The uses of those very powers and policies, or the choice of whether some should be used at all, go to the very core of independence. Lévesque himself recognizes this whenever he talks about the same powers and policies in other connections.

If I were a negotiator for Quebec, I would certainly want to aim at having and keeping power over taxation, social policies, borrowing policies and other economic matters. Or if I were a negotiator for Canada, I would feel the same way about protecting Canada's independence. I would be afraid for Quebec to have sovereign powers whose use could jeopardize Canadian currency, yet I would see no point in Quebec's having sovereign powers if it were not going to use them. And

I would reason much the same way if I were a negotiator for Quebec.

Lévesque's general remarks on currency, in his book and in the press conference he held after the White Paper was tabled, seem to indicate that he became a fan of the Bretton Woods agreement at some time in the past, when it deceptively appeared to be working, and has not given the question further careful thought in recent years. His comments, including those on European currencies, are out of date. Bretton Woods, before its messy breakdown, was supposed to lead to a shared European currency. Of course, it has led to no such thing, but Lévesque still does not seem to understand that the members of the European Economic Community have excellent reasons for not having proceeded as they originally planned. Now and again in his book he chides them for not doing so.

Lévesque introduces his thoughts on currency by saying: "As you know, this subject belongs in an area about which, as a whole, public opinion very easily becomes nervous. There is an aura almost of black magic to the word 'monetary.' " The impression I get is that Lévesque himself is easily made nervous by the subject. Here I am conjecturing, but perhaps this is because he feared that derogatory remarks about the probable value of a Quebec currency could easily be used to panic people in Quebec, no matter how ill-founded or unfounded the slurs might be.

Be that as it may, two of the things Lévesque wanted for Quebec—independence and a shared currency with the rest of Canada—are simply irreconcilable. Is there any way around this?

The experience of Ireland suggests a possibility. To see why, we must make a brief and sketchy sortie into some Irish economic history. When Ireland wrested its independence from Britain in 1922, it wanted free trade with Britain and it also wanted its own currency and central bank. Britain would agree on free trade, but only if Ireland agreed to keep the pound. Of course, Ireland did not participate, in the years that followed, in British decisions that either directly or indirectly helped influence the fate of the pound. And, of course, Ireland itself was so small a part of imperial Britain that nothing done by Ireland could much affect the value of the pound. But because Ireland had wanted its own money, for reasons of pride if nothing else, a fiction was arranged. Irish coins were minted, very handsome coins with their own pictures: harps, pigs, sailboats. No British royalty on them. Bills were printed and called the Irish pound. But the Irish pound was the British pound by a different name, just as the Scottish pound is to this day. The Irish coins were British coins with different pictures. The Bank of Ireland was a branch of the Bank of England.

In 1973 Ireland joined the European Economic Community, but the Irish pound remained the British pound. Then in January 1979 an interesting thing happened: Ireland joined the European Monetary System and Britain did not. That move severed the Irish pound from the British pound. Now Ireland had its own currency in fact; the new, independent unit of currency was named the Irish punt.

Under the European system, national currencies now float against one another, fluctuating up and down within certain specified ranges for each. When a given currency transgresses those limits, the central banks buy or sell it in large quantities, whichever is appropriate; this is to guard against wild fluctuations that otherwise might be triggered by speculations in currency. Of course, similar devices are used, when central banks think they are needed, to calm down the U.S. dollar, the Canadian dollar, the British pound and various other currencies as well. Every so often in Europe, when it is clear that

realities of production, trade and rates of inflation are changing, the ranges of float for various currencies are altered so
they can continue to reflect realities. That lesson of Bretton
Woods has been learned.

When the new Irish punt joined the European Monetary
System in January 1979, it was assigned a range of fluctuations
through which it was expected to float, below the value of the
British pound. The punt did drop very briefly to 91 British
pence. But then it swiftly rose in value and hovered close to
the top of the fluctuation range assigned to it, much to the
surprise of many experts. Throughout 1979 the punt's value
remained close to 97 British pence, which is as if the Canadian
dollar had been worth 97 U.S. cents instead of the 84 or 85
cents which was its usual value during the year.

Even more interesting has been the punt's stability.
Throughout the year it remained more stable than the British
pound itself. Although the punt is a minor currency—the
population of Ireland is less than half the size of Quebec's,
after all—it has behaved like Europe's strong currencies, as
one expert at the Bank of Canada's office in Toronto put it.

The Irish, obviously, had developed confidence that they
could depend on their own currency; otherwise they would
not have severed their connection with the British pound, for
the choice to do so was theirs.

My suggestion is this: if Canada and Quebec ever construct
a framework of sovereignty-association, it might best be done
in stages, like the way Norway achieved its self-government
and independence from Sweden—in stages. The complete
framework of sovereignty-association might require too much
adjustment for either Quebec or Canada to make at one time.
If the changes were made progressively, then during the period when Quebec was in process of achieving more autonomy and independence, it could arrange a fictional currency

like the old Irish pound. This would actually be a shared currency—that is, Canadian currency under a different name. Then, in due course, as Quebec gained both independence and self-confidence, it could convert the symbolic currency to its own actual currency, much as the Irish have done.

Fluctuations in currency can be helpful, especially between close trading partners. It depends, of course, on what causes the fluctuations. If the causes are changes in trade balances, then fluctuations can work very well as correctives. That is, when a country begins to run a deficit in what it sells relative to what it buys, it is paying out to other nations more money than it is taking in. Other nations have an oversupply of its money, and its exchange value drops. That drop means the country's exports automatically become cheaper to foreign buyers. Thus the drop in exchange value can help a small country boost and diversify its export trade precisely at the moment when the boost and diversification are needed. A drop in exchange value also means imports become more expensive. And this can help stimulate the country to replace some imports by locally made goods, again precisely at the moment when the stimulation is most needed.

But in a big country like Canada, embracing many and widely differing regions, currency fluctuations cannot serve these corrective purposes the way they can in a small country. That is because one region may badly need its exports boosted at the same time that trade surpluses in the country—taken as a whole—are pushing up the value of the Canadian currency; therefore, exports of the region in trouble become more expensive to foreign buyers, not cheaper, which is the help needed at the moment. The reverse also happens; a region with a trade surplus must pay more heavily for imports than it would have to if its own currency were at work. The more important the foreign trade of a region, relative to domestic trade, the more serious and the more economically harmful to a regional economy these contradictions can be. Since so many of Canada's regions depend so heavily upon foreign trade—exporting their resources, buying back foreign manufactured goods—they are especially vulnerable to the contradictions between the help they need from exchange fluctuations and the actual behavior of the currency.

Canada thus embodies a serious economic difficulty, built right into it. The value of Canadian currency that may be beneficial at a given time to Ontario may be harmful to British Columbia and Saskatchewan. The value beneficial to Quebec may, at the same moment, be harmful to New Brunswick. All this is nobody's "fault." Rather, it would be a miracle if the currency's exchange value at a given time were actually beneficial across the whole country.

If in due course an independent Quebec acquired a currency of its own, Quebec would have a built-in economic advantage it now lacks, an advantage that countries like Norway and Ireland have. That would not solve the problem of Canada's less sensitive currency, but at least it would help a little by diminishing the range of regions our Canadian currency must try to serve so clumsily.

EIGHT

Sovereignty-Association: Independence

Quebec is the only province for which independence is realistically possible in the foreseeable future. The chief reason is equalization. Under our equalization policies, federal tax yields from all the provinces, rich and poor, are pooled, then redistributed. They help pay for public services and social programs that poor provinces could not maintain on their own. In addition, Ottawa tries to help out the poor provinces with special, and usually very expensive, development schemes intended to attract or subsidize industry.

Equalization has been made necessary by the huge discrepancies of wealth and poverty between the provinces. In theory, equalization has not been intended merely as charity, but rather as a collection of social and economic programs supposed to improve the economies of poor provinces directly or indirectly, and thus help them become more self-supporting. But it has not really worked out that way. The poor provinces remain poor. Nevertheless, the funds distributed through the good offices of Ottawa do make poverty easier to bear and do help gloss over economic stagnation in the poor provinces.

The poorest are the Atlantic Provinces, but Saskatchewan

and Manitoba are also on the receiving side of the ledger. In federal-provincial conferences of recent years, premiers from Saskatchewan, Manitoba, New Brunswick, Nova Scotia, Prince Edward Island and Newfoundland have usually supported strengthened central government. Quite apart from the emotional attachments in these provinces to Confederation, strong federalism is their bread and butter. Recently exploratory drilling off Newfoundland has raised prospects of wealth from oil: in precise concert with those rising hopes, Newfoundland's premier has suddenly begun advocating weaker central government and greater provincial autonomy. The hopes being still unrealized, that policy is still tentative.

Ontario and Alberta are the two richest provinces, but British Columbia is also on the giving side of the ledger. In any conference of premiers, the leaders of these three provinces have usually pressed for greater provincial autonomy, more leeway to run their own affairs and make their own decisions, meaning looser federalism.

Neither the have-not provinces nor the haves are in a position to think seriously about independence. The have-nots are too dependent upon the federal government; the federal government is too dependent upon the haves. Ontario, Alberta and British Columbia are thus somewhat in the position of family breadwinners who have taken on heavy responsibilities for their dependents. They may complain about the burdens, they may grumble and insist on having their own way sometimes, but morally and practically they cannot walk out on their dependents. The dependents, for their part, may grumble and envy, may even accuse their benefactors of having trapped them into economic dependency. In particular, they often accuse Ontario of having done that. But the dependents cannot walk out.

The bookkeeping of equalization is so complex and confused that it is literally beyond understanding. And in addition to equalization payments, the federal government distributes other funds. The costs entailed by the military, judiciary, the CBC, transportation, forestry, fisheries and the terrible postal service are spent largely out in the provinces. Then there are various subsidies, such as those embedded in formulas of Central Mortgage and Housing and the Agriculture Department. There are foreign affairs expenses and the costs of the national debt for which each province theoretically owes its fair share, and so on.

Nobody, whether in Ottawa or in the provinces, knows exactly what the balance sheets are, exactly what the difference is between tax revenues sent from any given province to Ottawa, and the revenues and services received back. Even so, the discrepancies between what is yielded and what is received are great enough in nine cases so that there is no doubt about their financial roles in Confederation: three breadwinners, six dependents.

Quebec, the tenth, is a different case. The Quebec government has claimed that Quebec yields up more revenue to Ottawa than it gets back, and has made out plausible-sounding cases to support that claim. Ottawa, on the other hand, has said Quebec gets more than it yields and has made out plausible-sounding cases to support that claim too. The very fact that they can both argue this way shows how close the balance sheet must be. Walter Gordon has said that when he was federal finance minister in the early 1960s, Quebec had a quarter of the population, yielded just about a quarter of federal revenues and probably got back just about a quarter. Judy LaMarsh, in a political memoir covering the same period, has remarked, without elaborating, that Quebec was "not a have-not province," an impression she evidently derived as the federal cabinet minister entrusted with organizing Canada's social insurance system. Things may have changed since; nobody really knows.

Both Lévesque and Ryan purport to know. The introductory material to the Ryan constitutional proposals states that Quebec alone gets almost half of all Canada's equalization payments, but the claim can be substantiated only by including certain categories of federal payments and ignoring all the others. Lévesque says that Quebec pays in about a quarter of the federal government's revenues and gets back only about 15 percent, but again, this can be substantiated only by dwelling on certain categories of payments and ignoring or touching lightly on all the others. Ryan's object is to emphasize to Quebecois the financial advantages to them of remaining in Canada; Lévesque's aim is to emphasize the financial advantages of sovereignty. Quebec's current finance minister, Jacques Parizeau, a member of Lévesque's cabinet, says that before 1974 the balance sheet was equal, and that since then Quebec has been receiving more than it pays out; however, the discrepancy is owing only to oil-price subsidies and amounts to the value of a dozen pints of beer per person annually. Robert Bourassa, the previous premier, who like Parizeau is an economist, says the balance sheet is still equal, that figures can back either argument, and that it is of no importance, anyway, because Quebec should "remain in Canada to share in its immense store of natural resources."

Whatever may be the exact truth concealed beneath the impenetrable bookkeeping, the point is that Quebec is singular. It is the only province that could become independent without forcing financial sacrifices on either the other provinces or itself. In the future, of course, that could change. If Quebec remains a province indefinitely and Montreal declines into a typical Canadian regional city, Quebec will become a serious financial burden on the breadwinning provinces.

Sovereignty is many-sided. Its various aspects overlap and interlock. Keeping that in mind, we can think, however, of Lévesque's proposals for a sovereign Quebec as falling into three broad groups: cultural sovereignty, economic sovereignty and political sovereignty.

Cultural sovereignty revolves around language. That is to be expected because language is at the heart of any people's culture. What Lévesque wants culturally for Quebec is powers concerned with communications, immigration and language. He defines communications as television and radio broadcasting. He wants a Quebec broadcasting company independent from the Canadian Broadcasting Corporation, which under that name now produces English-language programs and under the name Radio Canada produces programs in French. As for immigration, he says that for generations "the federal government has maintained a very active network of immigration offices in England, Scotland and Ireland, while there has never been one in France."

When he speaks of the language question directly, he regrets that "a fortress of laws," as he puts it, has been necessary to protect the rights of Quebecois to use their own language professionally and in their general participation in Canadian life. He says one of the reasons he has dreamed of political sovereignty is "precisely so that we will not have to legislate on questions which should be as clear as the air we breathe." In matters concerned with language, he has wanted Quebec to have, as he puts it, whatever is normal to a national community which administers its own affairs.

As to whether this is a good or bad cultural aim, I for one cannot help but think it is good. While I have been writing this, I have been entertaining myself at the end of the day's work by reading the translation of a charming Japanese novel, by Ogai Mori, written in 1913 about the Japan of the 1880s, and a novel about the pageant of English history, by Virginia Woolf. I love living these multiple lives. It is possible only because many different cultures have become marvelously articulate, enriching our own culture and enriching me. For the culture of French Quebec to languish rather than flourish on its own terms—which is the only way any culture can flourish—would mean some impoverishment for us all.

But those sentiments do not specifically tell us why Lévesque and many other Quebecois have now become so aggressive about the elbowroom their culture needs. The most thoughtful comments I have come across are those of David Cameron, a political scientist who now works for the federal government as an expert on Quebec. He points out that before the "quiet revolution" of the 1960s, the culture of French Quebec had managed to preserve itself behind a shell of isolation and unchanging tradition. It did little more than survive, but in isolation it found the security to do that. Now, he points out, there is no security for the culture in resistance to change. Too much else has changed. The only possible security for Quebec's culture since 1960 has been to initiate changes in its own right and ride with them. It has to develop or die.

Cameron and the authors he quotes have some interesting things to say about views concerning uniformity and diversity, and I am going to comment on this point because it has a bearing not only on cultural sovereignty but also on economic sovereignty.

A few paragraphs back, I remarked that every different articulate culture enriches us all. That is such a cliché that we might suppose it has always been self-evident. Not so. It expresses a rather recent point of view.

During what we call the Enlightenment—the European intellectual climate that prevailed during the eighteenth century and that extended, in many ways, well into Victorian times—

people took a view of nature which has since been turned upside down. The Enlightenment view was that nature itself seeks standardization, uniformity, universality, immutability. Spinoza, a forerunner of the Enlightenment, put it in so many words: "The purpose of Nature is to make men uniform, as children of a common mother." People always seem to want to believe they are in harmony with the world as it is ordered by nature or the gods that be. Perhaps such a belief is necessary to human morale. At any rate, any civilization's conception—at the time—of natural order seems to wriggle into people's thoughts about all kinds of things, and so it was with the thought of the Enlightenment. Universality and uniformity, as ideals, subtly influenced how people thought about education, politics, economics, government, everything.

In the meantime, naturalists went on studying nature and its ways. What they found made it impossible to continue thinking of nature as a force promoting uniformity. On the contrary, what they found in nature was a force forever hostile to uniformity, a force that insisted upon diversity. Thus today we think of standardization, and immutability too, as being literally unnatural. An American paleontologist can now remark in passing, with every expectation of being understood by a general readership, that "new species almost always arise in tiny populations separated from larger parental groups," and he can go on to say that because of facts like that, evolutionary biologists like himself "tend to equate goodness with the correlation between unconstrained smallness and innovation and the sheer exuberant diversity of life."

As you may have noticed by now, that sort of view has worked a strong influence upon me; it did so long before I was conscious of its source in the thinking of naturalists. In this, I am a perfectly ordinary product of our civilization. As one cultural historian quoted by Cameron puts it, in the entire history of thought there have been "few changes in standards of value more profound and more momentous" than the shift from belief in natural uniformity to belief in natural diversity, a belief he sums up this way: not only are there diverse excellences in many, or in all, phases of human life, but "diversity itself is of the essence of excellence."

That idea has not yet been assimilated in all the nooks and crannies of our thoughts, let alone our actions. We still find many cultural lags. Nevertheless, the belief has already influenced thought and action in a thousand everyday ways. And we may be as sure as we can be sure of anything that as long as our current understanding of nature prevails, the belief that diversity itself is the source of vitality will continue to be a powerful and growing influence on thought about all kinds of things.

At the time the underlying cultural rules for Canada were laid down, the ideal of uniformity and universality was still operating full force. As a heritage, it has left us deeply uneasy about the separateness of English and French Canada and with a supposition that it represents some sort of social or political failure. That idea has been dinned into us by novelists and by politicians, and especially by the historians of English-speaking Canada. We are supposed to feel inadequate, somehow even guilty, for maintaining "two solitudes." Our mission, we were given to understand from way back, was to dissolve differences.

But looked at in the light of changed and changing ideas about uniformity and universality on the one hand and diversity on the other, the uneasiness and guilt are antiquated. Looked at in that light, the federal government's national bilingual policy is an instance of cultural lag, a sort of last gasp of the Enlightenment ideal. We force English-speaking civil servants with no gift for languages to qualify in French, and we legislate French and English for the labels on the bags of macaroni and for the announcements of postal rate increases, even where Italian and English, or Ukrainian and English, or Chinese and English, or Italian and French might be more to the point. If we have failed at uniformity—well, then, the bilingual policy tells us, we can still try for universality.

But once we have come to feel in our bones that diversity is valid, then the vision of an artificially bilingual Canada becomes simply arbitrary and silly. Then the separateness and dissimilarity between English and French Canada no longer seem cause for feelings of regret or failure on anyone's part. On the contrary, the whole stubborn tale comes to seem a triumph for the splendid principles of life itself. Lo and behold, here in our midst is dissimilarity that simply could not be squelched, and that now is insisting on its right to flourish. Three cheers for the dogged persistence and mysterious vitality of diversity.

An important practical virtue of diversity in human affairs is this: many truly independent institutions, even those with similar purposes, are bound to use different ways of going at things and are bound to develop different aims from one another too. With uniform or centralized control, improvements in human affairs come hard, and eventually come not at all. The chance of hitting on fresh ideas and fresh methods is thus the chief value of Lévesque's proposals for economic sovereignty.

Most of those proposals concern investment, ownership and control. Lévesque has wanted Quebec savings and other capital to be invested in Quebec's development. He would thus apply to Quebec much the same rule for control of banks that is now applied by Canada to Canadian banks. That is, nonresidents of Quebec would be permitted to hold no more than 25 percent of the voting shares of a bank operating in Quebec.

Similarly, Canadian law now requires Canadian insurance companies to reinvest fixed ratios of their incomes in Canada. Lévesque would leave the ratios undisturbed, but the insurance companies operating in Quebec would have to reinvest in Quebec. By these means he would attempt to stem what he calls the hemorrhaging of Quebec capital. His name for this policy is "repatriation" of the Quebec economy.

Behind that idea are many specific worries he expresses. He worries about Quebec's huge borrowings from outside the province and the country, and about the huge costs of servicing such debts. Those interest payments drain money away. He worries that so many Quebec industries and resources are owned and controlled from outside—sometimes because Quebec savings, lent abroad, return as foreign capital under foreign control.

He also worries over Canadian agricultural policies, about which he has this to say: "The Federal Minister of Agriculture very often follows policies which to us are undesirable and which sabotage the Quebec agricultural markets. This is the case very frequently in the milk industry, which is traditionally the backbone of Quebec agricultural production and which feels itself literally strangled."

Many people in other parts of Canada are, of course, worried about much the same things as Lévesque. They worry that Canada has become perhaps the largest borrower of foreign funds in the Western world; that almost half of Canadian manufacturing capacity is owned by U.S. companies; that Canada lacks venture capital or else does not know how to use it; that Canada's share of manufactured goods in world trade keeps dropping.

As a consumer of Ontario's excellent and varied cheddar cheeses, I worry about the Milk Board too. Its policies of restricting milk production and of reducing allocations of milk for cheese, the press informs us, are rapidly destroying all but the largest Ontario cheese producers. I will not be happy with nothing but Kraft and Borden Ontario cheeses.

Lévesque's proposals for economic sovereignty are not concerned with concrete questions of how economies develop. Of course it takes more than money to develop economic life; it takes fresh and practical ideas about what to do with money, and persistence, resourcefulness and courage to make the new ideas work out as actual production of goods and services and as practicable solutions to practical problems. I regret that in Lévesque's discussion of Quebec's economy I find nothing to contradict the conventional Canadian idea that wealth is based on natural resources rather than on the inventiveness and other talents of people. Nor am I encouraged by the Lévesque government's policy pronouncements on scientific and technological research. They sound just like every other bureaucracy's pomposities and pretensions on this subject.

In that case, we may well ask, what would be the point of two economic sovereignties where there was one before? Where is there any practical value in this particular possibility of diversity?

But there *is* practical value in the possibility. In the first place, Quebec's repatriation of banking and of capital would actually amount to significant economic change. Quebecois are assiduous savers; by and large, they are probably the most thrifty segment of Canadian society. The province is for this reason outstanding as a source of capital accumulation. It is also, and long has been, outstanding as an exporter of capital placed under the stewardship of the five great national Canadian banks and the insurance companies. Lévesque says that from 1961 to 1975, Quebec "exported nine billion dollars net, which represents an enormous surplus for a society of six million people." Again, we must be suspicious of figures. This one, for example, does not separate export of Quebec savings from export of profits by enterprises owned by non-Quebec parent companies and stockholders outside Quebec. Furthermore, since Lévesque's definition of capital exports embraces funds lent in parts of Canada other than Quebec (as well as any deposited or lent in foreign countries), the figure can only be an estimate in any case, which is why it is such a round figure. There is no dispute, however, that Quebec is a considerable exporter of capital. Ottawa, the banks and Lévesque's political opponents have made no case to the contrary.

Quebec's repatriation of banking and capital would inescapably lead to some changes in use of capital there. We can see why by considering the case of a real estate developer who builds office buildings and makes a success of it. If he can go on putting up office buildings in city after city after city, he can repeat his same work endlessly. But if he is confined to working in one or two cities, he cannot (in most cases) keep endlessly repeating himself. The market at hand limits him. When it gets saturated, he has to turn to building for other uses.

The same principle applies to financing. Lenders who finance natural-resource projects can repeat themselves endlessly if they can finance such development anywhere over a four-thousand-mile stretch of the earth, and then repeat themselves from Montana to Brazil besides. The same applies to financing of standard consumer loans, condominiums, branch plants, whatever—the same uses of capital can be repeated endlessly. But if the geographic scope is greatly narrowed, those same lenders are virtually forced into more diverse financing. The money cannot be used productively in endless repetitions of the same things. Furthermore, such opportunities will necessarily appear different depending upon whether the lender views a grand continental perspective superficially or whether he looks at a smaller, specific territory in depth.

In the second place, the fact that different people would be in charge in the two different sovereignties of Quebec and Canada, and have two different constituencies, would increase the chances of fresh economic decisions and fresh economic approaches emerging. Finally, the fact that Quebec really does have a different culture means increased chances that things would be done somewhat differently there.

At worst, we in the rest of Canada would learn nothing useful should Quebec ever become an associated sovereignty; at best, we might learn a good deal. Even the federal Milk Board might conceivably learn something from the way Quebec would choose to regulate, or deregulate, its dairy industry.

Now we come to political sovereignty. With one exception, Lévesque's proposals on this subject are easily stated. He would like the Quebec National Assembly (which is the provincial parliament) to have the powers of a national parliament. For instance, it would have sovereignty over the collection of all Quebec taxes and their appropriation. He would like Quebec to have a seat in the United Nations and probably to retain membership in the Commonwealth.

All that is straightforward, and normal and simple enough, at least in concept. But whenever Lévesque touches on the subject of a formal structure for joint Canadian-Quebec affairs, his proposals become tortured and his comments ambivalent.

On the one hand, he expresses fears that direction of Quebec's affairs might revert back to Ottawa. And—in a remark apropos the European Economic Community—he expresses his fears that associated sovereignties face the danger of falling into what he calls "merely a multinational, multicultural federalism."

On the other hand, when he attempts to depict Canadian-Quebec cooperation on customs union and currency, he conjures up exactly the sort of centralized bureaucracy and power structure that would make his fears come true. He has proposed joint bodies at what he calls the technocratic level, centralized ministerial structures, possibly also "a delegated parliament to which both sides would delegate members who are already elected to their parliaments, and which would meet once or twice a year . . ."

And then he adds: "It could go further if necessary, but on one condition: that, when the time comes, sovereignty in all its defined dimensions is neither affected nor restricted by exterior structures." Indeed? Then why have all those exterior structures?

The Quebec government's White Paper conjured up an even more elaborate superstructure, rearing itself above the present federal government in Ottawa. Quebec proposed not only a joint council of ministers for the two countries, and a commission of experts to act as a general secretariat for both Canada and Quebec, but also two central banks, one for Canada and one for Quebec, which in some matters would act on their own and in other matters would act jointly under yet another superfederal body, a monetary authority. Still another body, a court of justice, would have jurisdiction over interpretation and implementation of the treaties that set up the supergovernment and over the supergovernment's actions. The court's decisions would be final and binding on both Canada and Quebec. If, in addition to all this, the rest of Canada might want a superinterparliamentary assembly for the two countries, Quebec proposed that too as a matter for negotiation. All this reminds one of Ryan's constitutional proposals for duality.

In the preceding chapter I explained why two of Lévesque's aspirations for Quebec—independence, and a shared currency with Canada—are not reconcilable. Here we see the contradiction again. The proposed supergovernment would be necessary precisely for joint control of matters affecting a shared currency. But it is at odds with the kind of political structure appropriate to the sovereignty Lévesque has wanted for Quebec—or indeed to sovereignty for the rest of Canada. It is compatible, instead, with "merely a multinational, multicultural federalism," to use Lévesque's own description of what should be avoided. And it would saddle us all with additional, complex and expensive layers of bureaucracy and a new layer of centralized control beyond anything we have now. This would be too high a price to pay for what I can only understand as Quebec's timidity concerning a currency of its own.

In sum, then, looking at sovereignty-association as a whole, while Lévesque's concept seems to offer much that would be advantageous to both Canada and Quebec, it is also flawed, and the flaw is so important that it would undercut all the potential advantages for Canada and most of those for Quebec.

Does the defect mean that sovereignty-association should be dropped as a possibility? No, not at all. Here I will offer a fable which happens to be true. Some years ago the Ontario government joined with a West German corporation in a joint venture, the object being to develop a new form of transit—quiet, very rapid and efficient in its requirements for both energy and space. Electromagnets were used to move the vehicles without friction on a cushion of air above a narrow elevated track. Unfortunately, the thing would not work on curves. After some $25 million had been spent, Ontario and its German partner dropped the project and wrote it off. Who'd want a train that can't turn corners?

The Japanese did. Japan Airlines took up the idea and spun off a new enterprise (a mutation) to work on the project, on the premise that even if the track had to be straight, good uses could still be found for the system. That was reported in the Toronto press, along with the comments of an Ontario transportation expert who had visited the first Japanese test track. He said it was "so straight it's almost unbelievable," and that the absence of curves "simplified the project enough to enable the Japanese to get going." Soon after that was published in the summer of 1979, further word reached Toronto from the head of the Japanese project's engineering group. He reported that they had found a way, after all, to overcome the problem of curves. Test vehicles were now running successfully, he said, on two curvilinear sections of track.

The moral, of course, is that you do not start with what you cannot do. You start with what you can do, if the doing has worthwhile advantages. Then, if you can, you evolve improvements on that foundation. This is the commonsense approach to all creative endeavors of any difficulty. Indeed, it amounts to virtually a law of development, whether we are thinking of the way things are successfully developed by human beings or of the way development takes place in nature.

Lévesque's concept has a flaw, but if it is ever adopted, it can do other useful things. Independence, or sovereignty, would in any case have to be introduced in Quebec in steps and stages. By the time it became necessary to confront the need for a separate currency, Quebec might well have built up the necessary self-confidence to have one. Technically, the problem is not nearly as difficult as putting those curves in the track, nor is introduction of a new currency for a new sovereignty an unprecedented sort of problem. It has often been done successfully.

All of us, if we are reasonably comfortable, healthy and safe, owe immense debts to the past. There is no way, of course, to repay the past. We can only pay those debts by making gifts to the future. We are all worried, I think, about our bequests to the future—worried that we may be presenting the generations to come with heavy burdens rather than new gifts.

Among the burdens we have contrived are the stifling, wasteful and all but uncontrollable centralized bureaucracies that have proliferated so wildly and rapidly in our time, even in Canada. What a mess. What a load for the next generations to bear.

Perhaps in due course, in Canada, we could do a little something to lighten that burden. If we were eventually to work out a kind of sovereignty for Quebec, and a kind of association that really does combat centralization instead of increasing it, that would be a presentable gift to the future.

Nobody has quite done what we would have to do: sort out and keep only the connections Quebec and the rest of Canada would need to trade with each other and cooperate on projects of mutual interest, and discard the connections that would require Quebec and the rest of Canada to try to run each other's government as well as its own. If we could do that, we could say what people say of the gifts they are proudest to give: "We made it ourselves."

It could be our way of answering a question that Virginia Woolf has posed like this:

"Look at ourselves, ladies and gentlemen! Then at the wall; and ask how's this wall, the great wall, which we call, perhaps miscall, civilization, to be built by orts, scraps and fragments like ourselves?"

References

ONE

The quotation beginning "Leaders of these new regimes . . ." is from *Nationalism, Self-Determination, and the Quebec Question,* by David Cameron (Canadian Controversy Series; Toronto, Macmillan of Canada, 1974).

The anguished comparison of Canada with the Austro-Hungarian Empire is from *Unfulfilled Union,* by Garth Stevenson (Canadian Controversy Series; Toronto, Macmillan of Canada, 1979).

TWO

Population growth comparisons are derived from census figures of Statistics Canada.

The quotation on Canadian inventions is from *Ideas in Exile,* by J.J. Brown (Toronto, McClelland and Stewart, 1967). This is a basic work for light on the Canadian economy.

The economy's reliance on branch plants, which I have summarized, and the attitudes behind it are exhibited in the press almost daily. A commonplace example from the Nelson (B.C.) *Daily News* (January 22, 1980) quotes one of British Columbia's senior civil servants, the Deputy Minister of Forests: "If we export this inexpensive [hydroelectric] power, we make it attractive for firms to locate in Washington and Oregon. If we kept the cheap power here, perhaps companies would move to B.C. and create employment here."

Two important recent books illuminating the subject of Canadian economic attitudes are: *The Arrow,* by James Dow (Toronto, James Lorimer, 1980), and *C. D. Howe, a Biography,* by Robert Bothwell and William Kilbourn (Toronto, McClelland and Stewart, 1979).

Figures on the losses entailed in grandiose failures are from: "How ITT Got Lost in a Big Bad Forest," by Carol J. Loomis, *Fortune* (December 17, 1979).

Personal communication, Atomic Energy of Canada, Ottawa.

Personal communication, Ontario provincial research staff, New Democratic Party, Toronto, and Atomic Energy of Canada.

Dow, *op. cit.*

The *Globe and Mail,* Toronto (February 8 and 12, 1980).

The quoted phrase "a sad tale . . ." is from *René, a Canadian in Search of a Country,* by Peter Desbarats, rev. ed. (Seal Books; Toronto, McClelland and Stewart—Bantam Ltd., 1977).

THREE

The historical information on Norway and Sweden is from the following:

A History of Modern Norway 1814–1972, by T. K. Derry (Oxford, Clarendon Press, 1973).

A Brief History of Norway, by John Midgaard (Oslo, Johan Grundt Tanum Förlag, 1969).

A History of Norway, by Karen Larsen (Princeton N.J., Princeton University Press, 1948).

One Hundred Norwegians, edited by Sverre Mortensen and Per Vogt (Oslo, Johan Grundt Tanum Förlag, 1955).

FOUR

Data on Canadian-Norwegian trade are from Government of Canada, Department of Industry, Trade and Commerce, Western Europe Division; and Statistics Canada, Imports and Exports between Norway and Canada for the years 1976–1978.

Information on Norway's recent developments in manufacturing are from:

New Norway, edited by Gunner Jerman for the Export Council of Norway (Oslo, Gröndahl and Son, 1973).

Norway 79, edited by Gunner Jerman (Oslo, Export Council of Norway, 1979).

Facts About Norway, edited by Ola Veigaard, 15th ed. (Oslo, Aftenposten 1975).

Personal communication, Norwegian Trade Commission, Toronto.

Historical information on Nova Scotia is from *A History of Nova Scotia,* by G. G. Campbell (Toronto, Ryerson Press, 1948), and personal communication, Bank of Nova Scotia.

The report on the grocers' difficulties is from the *Globe and Mail,* Toronto (January 16, 1980).

FIVE

Information on the Chrysler Corp. is from numerous news stories in the *Wall Street Journal,* New York, throughout 1979.

Information on Standard Oil's dissolution is from *History of Standard Oil,* by George Gibb and Evelyn Knowlton, Vol. 2 (New York, Harper's, 1956).

Information on the Canadian restaurant industry is from personal communication, Ontario Hostelry Directorship Institute, Toronto.

The nursery rhyme may be found in *The Oxford Dictionary of Nursery Rhymes,* edited by Iona and Peter Opie (Oxford, Clarendon Press, 1952); a splendid book.

The essay by J.B.S. Haldane is to be found in *The World's Best Essays,* edited by F. H. Pritchard (New York, Albert and Charles Boni, 1932).

Comment by Marshall McLuhan concerning decentralization: personal communication.

SIX

The Ryan proposals are from *A New Canadian Federation,* by the Constitutional Committee of the Quebec Liberal Party; full English translation, the *Globe and Mail,* Toronto (January 10, 1980).

Biographical material on René Lévesque is from *René,* by Desbarats; see citation in references under Chapter Two.

Characterization of Ryan has been put together from press reports and communication with some of his acquaintances.

The Mutt and Jeff quotation is from "Are Mutt and Jeff at Work?," by J. D. Morton, the *Globe and Mail,* Toronto (December 14, 1979).

Analysis of the Quebec vote is from half a dozen public opinion polls; all agreed, including one by Carleton University, Ottawa, for which sample voters were questioned as to how they had voted, as they left the polls.

SEVEN

All references to Lévesque's ideas, except where otherwise noted, are from:

My Quebec, by René Lévesque, based on interviews conducted by Jean-Robert Leslbaun, English translation by Gaynor Fitzpatrick (Toronto, Methuen, 1979).

The White Paper on sovereignty-association is titled *Quebec-Canada: A New Deal—the Quebec Government Proposal for a New Partnership between Equals: Sovereignty-Association;* tabled in the Quebec National Assembly, November 1, 1979. I used the English translation published in full in the *Globe and Mail,* Toronto (November 2, 1979).

Information on interprovincial trade in manufactured goods is from Statistics Canada, Manufacturing and Primary Industries Division.

Information on the Irish punt is from personal communication with the Bank of Canada, the Irish Board of Trade in Toronto, and routine foreign exchange figures in the *Wall Street Journal*, New York.

EIGHT

Lévesque's ideas: see note under Chapter Seven.

The comment on the Quebec-Ottawa financial balance by Walter Gordon is from personal communication. That by Judy LaMarsh is from *Memoirs of a Bird in a Gilded Cage* (Toronto, McClelland and Stewart, 1968). The various viewpoints in dispute over this question are drawn from Lévesque's *My Quebec* (see citation under Chapter Seven), from the Ryan proposals (see citation under Chapter Six) and from a report in the *Globe and Mail*, Toronto (January 23, 1980).

Comment by David Cameron: see citation under references for Chapter One.

The cultural historian quoted by Cameron is A. O. Lovejoy, *The Great Chain of Being* (Harper Torchbooks; New York, Harper & Row, 1963).

The American paleontologist is Stephen Jay Gould, in *The New York Review of Books* (October 11, 1979).

The information on the Japanese transportation project is from the *Globe and Mail*, Toronto (July 25, 1979), quoting Morrison Renfrew, project manager for Ontario's Urban Transportation Development Corp.; and from a letter to the editor by Shinji Nakamura, Head, HSST System Engineering Group, Tokyo, published in the *Globe and Mail*, Toronto (September 1, 1979).

The quotation from Virginia Woolf is from *Between the Acts* (London, Hogarth Press, 1941; paperback edition: Harmondsworth, U.K., Penguin Modern Classics, 1974).

Index

agricultural policies of Canadian government, independent Quebec and, 116

Åland, Finland's rejection of independence for, 5–6

Alberta
oil in, 60
vis-à-vis Norway, 60

Asbjörnsen, Peter Christen, 36–37

Atlantic Provinces Chamber of Commerce, 95

Austro-Hungarian Empire, dissolution of, argument against Quebec independence and, 6–7

balance sheet on Canadian equalization payments, separatism and, 109–10

balance of trade
Canada and Norway, national policies effecting, 100
deficits, United States', international impact of, 98–100

"Balkanization," issue of, as applied to Quebec separatism, 6

Bangladesh, fight for independence, 6

banking, in independent Quebec, 115

Bank of Nova Scotia, 59

banks, two central, political sovereignty of Quebec and problem of, 120

beige paper, 86

borrowing and servicing debts, independent Quebec and, 116

Bourassa, Robert, 110

bilingual policy of Canadian federal government, as cultural lag, 114–15

branch plant nature of Canadian manufacturing industry, 19–20, 22, 24, 61

Bretton Woods agreements on international currencies, 97–99, 102, 104

British North American Act, 38, 78

Brown, J.J., 18

Calgary, as regional city, 21

Cameron, David, 112, 113

campaign on separatist referendum, 88

Canada
borrowing and servicing debts, 116
as branch plant economy, 19–20, 22, 61
colonial economy of, 54–55
constitution of, 78–89
cultural rules of universality and uniformity, 114
currency fluctuations and, 105–106
economic direction of, 100
economic development of, Norway and, 53–56
economic life, customary view of, 16–18
energy industry, 56
federalism in, 76
innovations in economic spending, failure of, 18
as importing country, problems of, 19
manufacturing in, 19–20
metric conversion, as gimmick to economic development, 63–64
Norway's independence from Sweden, lessons for, 26–51
regional cities, role of, 20–21
restaurant work in, 67–68
wealth, view of, 17
trade with Norway, 55

Canadian Broadcasting Corporation, 62, 111

Canadian-Norwegian trade, size of nation and, 55

Canadian-Quebec affairs, problems of, in Lévesque's views on political sovereignty, 119–21

Candu, 18

capital
accumulation in Quebec, 117
export by Quebec, 117–18
use of, by independent Quebec, 118–19

Catholic Church in Quebec, 13

Chrysler Corporation, paradox of size and, 65–66, 67, 69

cities of Canada, economic structure of, 20–21

citizenship, dual, between Canada and Quebec, 96

Collett, Camilla *(The Country Governor's Daughter)*, 37
communications, Quebec's control of, 111
complications due to size of political entity, 70–77
  federalism and, 76–77
  Lake Ontario clean-up, case of, 74
  Metropolitan Toronto, case of, 73
  postal service, as example of, 74–75
  red tape, 73–74
  telephone service and, 75
"connurbation" of Toronto, 14–15
constitution of Canada, problems in, 78–79
  amending process, 78
  defeat of referendum on separatism and, 89
  duality proposal, 79–80
  Federal Council proposal, 81–83
  federal-provincial conferences on, 80
  insolubility of dual federalism, 89
  Quebec's role in, 79
  repatriating, 78–79
  Ryan amendment proposal, 80, 81–82
  Victoria Conference (1971) on amending and repatriating, 78, 79
  See also duality proposals for Canadian federalism
court of justice, political sovereignty of Quebec and, 120
Creation, Man and Messiah (Wergeland), influence of, on Norwegian independence movement, 33
cultural-economic nexus, separatism and, 21–22
cultural sovereignty of Quebec, 111–15
  benefits of, 111–12
  bilingualism and, 114–15
  Cameron's views on, 112
  Enlightenment and, 112–13
  language rights and, 111
  immigration and, 111
  naturalist's view and, 113
  uniformity and diversity, 112–15, 117
currency, separate, 122
currency, sharing same, as Lévesque's proposal for sovereignty-association, 97–105
  Bretton Woods agreement, 97–98, 102, 104
  Canadian currency difficulty, 106
  errors of proposal, 101

  fluctuations in currency, 105
  foreign trade-currency fluctuations, contradictions of, 105–106
  independence, problem of, 101–102
  inflation, international, 98–99
  Irish example, as possible solution, 102–105
  national policies and, 99–100
customs union, between Quebec and Canada, 96

De Gaulle, Charles, 4
development, law of, 122
diversity and uniformity, culture and, 112–15, 117
  value, 115
divisions, constant, in large nations, question of inevitability and desirability of, 67–69
dollars, depreciation of, international currencies and, 99
duality proposals for Canadian federation, 79–89
  beige paper on (Ryan's), 86
  cultural, 81
  defeat of referendum on separatism and, 89
  Federal Council proposal, 81–83
  judicial, 81
  "renewed federalism" promise of Trudeau, 88–89
  See also constitution of Canada

economic development
  gimmicks and shortcuts to development, 63–64
  national population and marketing potential, 52–53
  strategies of, 60
  versatility at production, 60–61
  See also national size, economic development and
economic nationalists, manufacturing and, 20
economic power shift from Montreal and Toronto, 14–16
economic sovereignty of Quebec, 115–19
  agricultural policies, 116
  banking, 115
  benefits of, 117–18
  borrowing and servicing debts, 116
  capital export in Quebec, 117–18
  development of economies, 117
  foreign capital problem, 116
  insurance companies, 116
  lessons for other provinces, 119

originality in economic planning, 119
scientific and technological research, 117
use of capital, 118–19
wealth, theory of, 117
economy, Canadian, nature of, 16–23
Edmonton, as regional city, 21
Eidsvold, town of, 28
emotion, as factor in separation question, 3–9
Austro-Hungarian Empire dissolution and, 6–7
"balkanization," 6
conflicts over identifying nation, 3–4
inconsistencies of positions, 4–6
"quiet revolution," 8–9
separatist sentiment, early history of, 7–8
uses of independence, 5–6
English supremacy over Quebec, 7–9
Englightenment, 112–13
equalization, Quebec independence and, 107
balance sheet of have's and have-not's, 109–10
bookkeeping of equalization, 108–109, 110
Lévesque's and Ryan's views, 110
poorer provinces and, 108
European Economic Community, 49, 53, 102, 103, 119
European Monetary System, 103, 104
Export Council of Norway's 1979 Annual, 56

Falconbridge Nickel, 55
Federal Council proposal to Canadian constitution, 81–83
federalism, complications of size and, 76–77
federalism, multinational and multicultural, problem of, in Lévesque's view of political sovereignty, 119, 121
poor provinces and, 108
sovereignty-association, problem of, 92–93
financial changes in Canada, 13–14
fluctuations in currency, 105
foreign capital, Quebec independence and, 116
foreign trade
Canada and Norway, national policies effecting, 100
currency fluctuations and, contradictions of, 105–106
free trade between associated sove-

reignties, as Lévesque's proposal for sovereignty-association, 93
free travel of persons, as Lévesque's proposal for sovereignty-association, 96

Golden Horsehoe, 15
Gordon, Walter, 109

Haldane, J.B.S., 70–71, 72, 77
Halifax
economic development of, 59
as regional city, 21
historical precedents of separatism, 5–7

Ibsen, Henrik, 39
immigration, Quebec's control of, 111
independence, sovereignty-association and, 107–23
cultural sovereignty, 111–15
economic sovereignty, 115–19
equalization, Quebec's independence and, 107–10
financial viability of Quebec independence, 110
laws of development and, 121–22
political sovereignty, 119–21
summary view, 121
See also sovereignty-association, connectors
inflation, international, common currencies and, 98–99
insurance companies in independent Quebec, 116
internal trade in Canada, sovereignty-association and, 94–96
Quebec and Ontario, 94–95
Quebec and provinces other than Ontario, 95–96
International Joint Commission for St. Lawrence Seaway, sovereignty-association and, 97
Ireland, problem of shared currency and, economic history of, 102–104

Japan Airlines, 121–22

LaMarsh, Judy, 109
language, Quebec's control of, 111
Le Devoir, 85
Lévesque, René, 21, 22, 83–84, 85, 87, 88, 91, 93, 96, 97, 100, 101, 102, 110, 111, 112, 115, 116, 117, 118, 119, 120, 121, 122
sovereignty-association, connectors (proposals for), 92–104

Liberal Party in Quebec, 83, 85, 86
  beige paper on separatism, 86
Louis Napoleon, 39

Macdonald, John A., 78
manufacturing in Canada, 53
  branch plant nature of, 19–20, 22,
    24, 53
  economic nationalism and, 19–20
maritime community on St. Lawrence
    River, as Lévesque's proposal for
    sovereignty-association, 97
Maritime Provinces, poverty of, 21, 24
McLuhan, Marshall, 75
Michelsen, Christian, 46–47
migration, intra-Canadian, to Toronto
    and Montreal, 15
military alliances, Quebec's participa-
    tion in, as Lévesque's proposal for
    sovereignty-association, 97
Milk Board of Canada, 119
mistakes, size of entity and conse-
    quences of, 69–70
Moe, Jörgen, 36–37
Montreal
  branch plants, 22
  capital needs of, 23–24
  economic changes in, sovereignty
    and, 10–16, 22–25
  economic growth, 11, 15–16, 20
  economic viability of, 23
  Frenchification of, 12
  growth of, 10–11, 13
  loss of power to Toronto, 14–16
  migration away from, Toronto and,
    15
  population statistics of, 14, 15
  "quiet revolution," 11
  as regional Canadian city, 16, 22–23
  role of, in Quebec separatism, 10–16
  rural goods and, 12
Montreal-Toronto nexus, issue of
    separatism and, 10–25. *See also*
    Montreal; Toronto
Mori, Ogai, 111–12
Morton, J.D., 86
Munch, P.A. *(History of the Norwegian
    People)*, 37
My Quebec (Lévesque), 93

nationalism, as emotional issue, 3–5
national size, economic development
    and, 52–64
  Canada, as colonial economy, 54–55
  Canada's domestic market, 53–54
  Canada's size, 62
  Canada *vis-à-vis* Norway, 57–58
  development, 61–62

gimmicks as development, 63–64
  Norway's economy, as example,
    55–62
  Nova Scotia, case of, 57–59
  Ontario fact sheet on, 53–54, 62
  versatility at production, 61
  See also size, paradoxes of
Navigation Acts, 34–35
Newfoundland, oil potential of, cen-
    tralized government and, 108
North Atlantic Treaty Organization,
    97
NORAD, 97
Norway
  coal and iron, 57–60
  Creation, Man and Messiah (Werge-
    land), effects on independence
    movement in, 33
  early poverty of, 30–31
  early separatists, 27–28
  economic direction of, 100
  economic relationship with Canada,
    55
  economy of, 52, 54–55
  economy, after independence, 49
  Eidsvold, town of, 28
  energy industry, 56
  fairy and folk tales of Moe and
    Asbjörnsen, influence of, 36–37
  history, 37–38
  industries of, 56–57
  linguistic dialects of, 35–36
  loss of independence, 27
  manufacturing in, 56–57
  mutant economic life in, 68–69
  Navigation Acts, British repeal of
    (1849) as influence on economy
    of, 34–35
  Nova Scotial shipbuilding and,
    57–58
  nynorsk (neo-Norwegian), 37
  oil in, 60
  population of, 52
  principles of economic develop-
    ment, 57–61
  Scandinavianization, impact of inde-
    pendence movement, 38–40
  shipping industry, 57–60
  technological research in, 56
  themes of independence, 32
  trade with Sweden, 49–50
  versatility at production, 60–61
  vis-à-vis Alberta, 60
  vis-à-vis Nova Scotia, 57–60
  See also peaceable secession, case of
    Norway seceding from Sweden
Nova Scotia, economy of (*vis-à-vis*
    Norway), in coal and iron, in ship-
    ping industry, 57–60

Ontario
   economic dependence of other prov-
      inces on, 108
   internal and foreign trade, 94
   population size of and marketing po-
      tential, 53–55
   trade with Quebec, 95

Parizeau, Jacques, 110
Parti Quebecois, 83–84, 86
   White Paper on Sovereignty-
      Association, 86
peaceable secession, case of Norway
   seceding from Sweden, 26–51
   Collett, Camilla *(The Country Gover-
      nor's Daughter)*, Norwegian fiction
      and, 37
   conflict and crisis between Norway
      and Sweden, 40–43
   consequences of separation, 48–50
   currency,   Swedish-Norwegian,
      31–32
   dissolution of union, 46–48
   early separatists in Norway, 28
   economic competition, foreign
      affairs and, 43–46
   Eidsvold Assembly, 28–29, 32
   Henrik Wergeland's influence, 32–
      33, 36
   independence strategy, 32
   Munch, P.A. *(History of the Norwegian
      People)*, development of Norwe-
      gian history by, 37
   Norwegian economy, 30–31
   Quebec separatism and, 50–51
   Scandinavianization, problem of,
      38–40
   shipping, Norwegian, economic in-
      dependence and, 34–35
   Storting (Norwegian parliament),
      29–30, 31, 33–34, 40–41
   Swedish governance of Norway,
      29–30
political   sovereignty   of   Quebec,
      119–21
   banks, two central, idea of, 120
   Canadian-Quebec cooperation and
      centralization, 119–20
   contradictions in Lévesque's view of,
      120–21
   court of justice, 120
   multinational, multicultural federal-
      ism, danger of, 119, 121
   Quebec National Assembly, powers
      of, 119
   superstructure for Canadian-Quebec
      affairs, 120–21
population, national, economic devel-
      opment through marketing poten-
      tial and, 52–54
   Ontario, case of, 62–63
   size   of   country   (*e.g.,*   Norway),
      61–62
   statistics of population growth and
      decline of Montreal and Toronto,
      14, 15
power and bigness of nation, 69
Prince Christian Frederick of Norway,
      28
productivity and monetary policies of
      nations,   common   currency
      proposals and, 99–100

Quebec City, 11
Quebec National Assembly, 119
Quebec, province of
   Canadian constitution and, 79–80,
      82
   capital accumulation in, 117
   capital export of, 117–18
   capital needs of, 22–24
   Catholic Church in, 13
   cultural sovereignty of, 111–15
   currency, independent, problems of,
      105–106
   economic culture of, 21–22
   economic sovereignty of, 115–19
   equalization   and   independence,
      107, 109–10
   under Federal Council proposal,
      82–83
   financial viability of independence,
      110
   Montreal's growth, as influence on
      culture of, 15–16
   non-Ontario trade, 95–96
   Norway's secession from Sweden,
      lessons of, 26–51
   political sovereignty of, 119–21
   referendum on separatism, 84–89
   rural, French culture and, 12
   separatist sentiment, history of,
      7–8
   sovereignty-association, problem of,
      92–93
   trade with Ontario, 95
   use of capital, if independent,
      118–19
"quiet revolution" in Quebec culture,
      8–9, 11, 12, 51, 112

Radio Canada, 111
referendum on separatism, Quebec,
      84–89
   outcome, 88
   wording of, 87–88
religious life in Quebec, 13

"renewed federalism" promise by Trudeau, 88–89
"repatriation" of Quebec economy, 116
restaurant work in Canada, 67–68
Rigsret (Supreme Court of Norway), 42
Ryan, Claude, 22, 80, 81, 83, 85–86, 87, 110, 120

St. Lawrence River, sovereignty-association and, 96–97
scientific research, Lévesque government's policy on, 117
separatist sentiment in Quebec, early history of, 7–8
size, paradoxes of, 65–77
  Chrysler Corporation, as example of, 65–66, 67, 69
  complexity and size, 70–77
  division, constant, principle of, 67–69
  "getting smaller," as advantage, 66
  Haldane's principle, 70–72, 77
  mistakes, consequences of, 69–70
  Standard Oil Company, 66–67
  See also national size, economic development and
sovereignty-association, connectors, 22, 90–106
  achieving in stages, 104–105
  currency, sharing same, as Lévesque's proposal for, 97–105
  domestic and international problem of, for nations, 91–92
  in federal systems, 92–93
  free trade between associated sovereignties, as Lévesque's proposal, 93–96
  free travel of persons, as Lévesque's proposal, 96
  governments and nations and, 91
  "independent"-"connected" elements, 90, 91
  as juggling act, 91–92
  Lévesque's proposals for, 92–104
  maritime community on St. Lawrence River, as Lévesque's proposal for sovereign-association, 97
  military alliances, Quebec's participation in, as Lévesque's proposal, 97
  synonyms for, 91
  wolf and deer analogy, 90–91
  See also independence, sovereignty-association and
Spinoza, Baruch, 113
Standard Oil Company, dissolution of, paradox of size and, 66–67
Statistics Canada, 93
Sverdrup, Johan, 41, 43
Sweden
  governing Norway, 29–30
  population of, 52
  trade with Norway, 49–50
  See also peaceable secession, case of Norway seceding from Sweden

taxation, common currency proposals and, 100
technological research, Lévesque government's policy on, 117
technology, Canadian, problems with, 18–19
Toronto
  "connurbation" of, 14–15
  economic growth, 14–15, 20
  as financial center of Canada, 13–14
  growth rate of, 14
  migration into, vs. Montreal, 15
  population statistics of, 14, 15
  power shift to, from Montreal, 14–16
  relationship to Montreal, 13–16
trade in Canada. *See* internal trade in Canada
trade items, Canadian, 55
Treaty of Kiel, 28
Trudeau, Pierre Elliott, 78–79, 88

uniformity and diversity, culture and, 112–15, 117
United States
  balance of trade deficit, international impact of, 98–99
  Canadian economy and, 54
  depreciation of dollar, 99
  as exporter of inflation, common currency proposals and, 98–99

Victoria Conference (1971), 78, 79

wealth, Canadian view of national, 17, 117
Wergeland, Henrik, 32–33, 36, 37, 48
White Paper on Sovereignty-Association (Liberal Party of Quebec), 86, 93, 97, 101, 102, 120
Winnipeg, as regional city, 21
Woolf, Virginia, 112, 123